Songs of the Saints
A Study of Selected Psalms

Songs of the Saints
A Study of Selected Psalms

John White, Jr.

This book has been prepared primarily for group study in connection with the Adult Teacher's Guide, available for $1.95 from Regular Baptist Press. A transparency packet with sixteen sheets is available for $6.95. This book may also be used for individual instruction.

REGULAR BAPTIST PRESS
1300 North Meacham Road
Post Office Box 95500
Schaumburg, Illinois 60195

About the Author

John White, Jr., is senior pastor of the Calvary Baptist Church, Grand Rapids, Michigan. Prior to assuming this pastorate in January 1967, Dr. White was a pastor in Iowa.

Dr. White earned the Th.B. degree from Baptist Bible College of Pennsylvania and the Th.M. from Dallas Theological Seminary. He was awarded the D.D. degree by Grand Rapids Baptist Theological Seminary. He is on the board of Grand Rapids Baptist College and Seminary and serves on the Council of Eighteen of the General Association of Regular Baptist Churches. Dr. White wrote *Arise and Build,* a series of adult Sunday School lessons on Ezra, for Regular Baptist Press. He is in great demand as a conference speaker.

Dr. White and his wife have two children. They reside in Grand Rapids.

Contents

© 1980 by Regular Baptist Press. Vol. 29, No. 2
Printed in U.S.A. Merle R. Hull, Executive Editor

Preface

THE BOOK OF PSALMS speaks clearly about the heartbeat and heartaches of men as they associated with their friends, families, a world of ungodly men and God. It reveals the varied feelings of the psalm writers: frustration, emptiness, victory, success, depression and mountaintop experiences. The writers put their reactions on paper as they journeyed the crooked and dangerous path of life. Your life will be enriched and challenged as you study these *Songs of the Saints*.

CHAPTER 1

Happy or Hopeless?

BIBLE PORTION TO READ: Psalm 1

A GROWING CONCERN in the United States today is the frustration caused by a rapidly moving, high-powered, hedonistic approach to life. Loud music, expensive recreational vehicles and thrill shows of every kind, coupled with an amoral attempt to capture happiness in discos and depraved relationships, have provided neither lasting happiness nor contentment. The emptiness of modern man's life cannot be disguised by sarcastic jokes, pills, pot, alcohol or immoral indulgence.

God's Word reveals the secret of happiness and contentment in Psalm 1.

The Happy Man

The word *blessed* in Psalm 1:1 is often translated "to be happy." What is happiness? For some people, happiness is associated with the "happy hour" at a cocktail lounge and is dependent upon externals. But the psalmist's word does not describe fickle, external, short-lived enthusiasm that leaves a bitter aftertaste. Rather, it speaks of an internal calmness and bliss that belongs to the person who knows that everything is right between himself and other people and between himself and God.

This blessedness belongs to the man who is situated on solid ground, the man who is free of remorse, guilt and emptiness because he is at peace with God. He is not seeking something he cannot find. He does not experience the sudden, terrible feelings that he ought to be somewhere doing something—that he is "missing out" in life. The blessedness he feels produces contentment and quietness, often accompanied by laughter or a smile. He can tolerate quiet places, loneliness and problems because he has an enduring reservoir of contentment and satisfaction. He has learned the meaning of the song "Happiness Is the Lord."

> Happiness is to know the Savior,
> Living a life within His favor,
> Having a change in my behavior,
> Happiness is the Lord.

David describes a different characteristic of the happy man in each of the first three verses of Psalm 1. The characteristic described in verse 1 is that he avoids evil. The characteristic in verse 2 is that he associates with the Word of God. The characteristic in verse 3 is that he attains a productive life.

The Happy Man Avoids Evil

A happy, contented man is one who avoids evil. Association with evil results in guilt, condemnation, breaking of fellowship, fear and passing the buck. Adam and Eve were two very happy people until they fell into sin by eating of the tree of the knowledge of good and evil.

8

Satan tempted them with the lie that eating of the tree would increase their knowledge, satisfaction and pleasure, but they discovered that they felt guilty instead. For the first time in their lives they felt like covering up. They could not face God, so they hid among the trees. And when God asked them what had happened, Adam blamed Eve, who in turn blamed the serpent. Their frustration and guilt have been repeated in every generation since then.

The Christian who avoids sinful practices and fellowship with sinners finds that contentment is lasting and that fellowship with God is sweet. Verse 1 tells us that the happy person is one who avoids evil counsel, the way of sinners and the place of the scorner. The result is the quiet happiness described by the word *blessed*.

The Happy Man Avoids Ungodly Counsel

The happy person is one who does not walk in the counsel of the ungodly; he is very careful where he gets his advice.

Mary Jones was a troubled woman. She had accepted the Lord Jesus Christ as a child, had grown up in a Christian home and had married a man who professed to know Jesus Christ as his Savior. After they were married, however, he refused to go to church with her, choosing rather to spend the day at home, working on the lawn or sitting in front of the television set. Mary went to church alone.

Her husband said that since she went to prayer meeting on Wednesday night, he would like to bowl on Thursday night. She consented to his night out "with the boys." That night out included a stop at the local bar from time to time. After two years of this, he often came home drunk.

As Mary became more and more distressed, it was difficult for her to pray or to read God's Word. She looked for a listening ear. The unsaved girl who worked next to her in the office was always ready to listen to her sad reports during lunch or coffee break. She had a worldly approach to life because her value system was not based upon the Word of God. She had just gone through a divorce.

As Mary talked with her about her problems, she offered sympathy and advice. She frequently made statements such as, "You would be better off without your husband. . . . Why do you put up with things like that? . . . I can tell you where you can find a good lawyer. . . . Divorce is better than depression. . . . I wouldn't take that from my old man. . . . You ought to press for a financial settlement before he squanders everything you own. . . . You have your rights!"

Mary listened to that kind of ungodly advice day after day. As she began to follow it, she found her life becoming barren and empty. Mary's face is drawn and often tearstained today because she is unhappily divorced, lonely and broken, having followed the advice of an ungodly woman.

The Happy Man Avoids the Sinner's Way

The second thing the psalmist says the happy man avoids is standing in the way of sinners. He maintains right priorities in his interests and activities. He does not position himself where sinners live and habitually spend their time.

The Smiths had a small English bulldog that loved to play games with the children. They would swing a stick or a cloth bag above his head. The dog would jump to grab the object with his teeth and then hang on as though his life depended on it. The children would lift him high into the air and swing him around their heads, but he would never let go.

One day Jimmy Smith took a dusty grain sack and began to swing it around the bulldog's head. As the dog grabbed the bag, the powdery ground wheat filtered into his mouth and up his nose. In typical bulldog fashion, however, he would not let go. Though he was sneezing and gagging, he continued to hang on for dear life. If bulldogs do much thinking, he was probably thinking, "I'll hang on if it kills me."

In the same way, some believers refuse to separate themselves from the place and position of ungodly people. As a consequence, they bring the problems of the ungodly into their own lives and experience the malcontent and discomfort that attend such association.

The Happy Man Avoids the Scorner

The third thing the happy man avoids is sitting in the seat of the scornful. He is not a part of the sarcastic sophistication that goes on around him, nor does he spend any time contriving sarcasm or mockery himself. He abides by the admonition of Ephesians 4:29: "Let no corrupt communication proceed out of your mouth, but that which is good to the use of edifying, that it may minister grace unto the hearers."

The Happy Man Loves God's Word

Pastor Dann Austin loves little children, and they are drawn to him as well. He is deeply involved in their lives and enjoys their presence. His pleasure is to know what they are thinking, how they feel and how they see their world.

In the same way, the man who is really happy is attracted to the Word of God. He delights in it and wants to spend time with it to know what God is saying and what His wishes are. He interacts with the Word of God, prays over it, commits it to his memory and applies its instruction to his life. Many people delight in sports magazines, health magazines, professional journals or even comic books. This kind of reading does not serve as a major magnetism to the contented Christian. His major interest is with God's holy Word.

> Holy Bible, Book divine,
> Precious treasure, thou art mine:

12

Mine to tell me whence I came,
Mine to teach me what I am;
. . . .
Mine to tell of joys to come
And the rebel sinner's doom:
O thou holy Book divine,
Precious treasure, thou art mine.

So intense is the contented person's interest in the Word of God that he actually thinks about it during the daylight hours and during the dark. He experiences the guidance, protection, conviction and discernment of God through His holy Word. The result of this is great quietness and joy.

The Happy Man Is Productive

The happy man attains a productive life. The psalmist illustrates this by talking about a tree. The tree described in verse 3 is one that has been uprooted by God and moved to a location that is best suited to productivity. God often finds it necessary to uproot the believer, to tear him away from the restraining forces of the community or job that were so much a part of his life before he knew Jesus Christ as his Savior. The believer is replanted in a setting where he can grow and mature in his faith.

A hundred years ago farmers and road builders went into the heavy timber to dig up small maple trees that struggled for sunlight under the dense leaves of the forest. They carried these trees to the edge of the roads or lanes and planted them in straight rows in the open sunlight. Having been thus transplanted, the young trees grew to enormous size and beauty. The happy man is one who has been uprooted and transplanted by God to a location where he can reach his full potential in service for God.

The psalmist says that this man is planted by the rivers of water, where he will receive all the moisture necessary for productivity. Notice that he brings forth his fruit when he is supposed to. He is not characterized by procrastination or defeat. He does what he is supposed to do when he is supposed to do it. Contentment comes with well-timed productivity.

David continues his analogy of the tree by saying that the godly man is productive in whatever he does—his leaves do not wither or fall. Remember, we are not speaking of prosperity in terms of worldly standards but in terms of God's standards. The man who is happy in his Lord will be productive at home, at work and in his ministry for the Lord Jesus Christ.

The Hopeless Man

The psalmist draws a startling contrast between the happy man and the hopeless man in this psalm. The hopeless man is an ungodly person who is likened to chaff. In David's day threshing floors were located on high places away from the trees so the wind could drive away the chaff. Grain was usually threshed and winnowed in the evening or at night when the breezes blew.

After beating the grain on the threshing floor, the threshers would throw it into the air. If the wind was blowing, the grain would fall back to the floor, but the chaff would blow away. If a farmer had very little grain to thresh, he simply permitted the chaff to blow across the fields to be plowed under. But if there was a lot of it, he burned it. The ungodly are like the chaff—unwanted, unneeded, nonproductive and headed for doom in eternal fire.

The emptiness and restlessness of fallen man

make him rush to try new adventures. He is continually building bridges that cross no chasms and erecting houses that hold no love. He saves for his old age but would rather die than live in the agony of his waning years. He struggles for the praise of people who betray him, works for money that is stolen from him and then dies to be forever forgotten by the betrayer and the thief.

In Isaiah 57:20 the fallen man is depicted as being like "the troubled sea, when it cannot rest, whose waters cast up mire and dirt." The opposing forces of gravity and the moon pull at the waters of the sea, causing it to ebb and flow. The winds blow billows and breakers that cause further movement. As a result the waters along the beaches are murky, and the beaches themselves are continually littered.

With man it is the same. The opposing forces of the world pull first one way then the next. The billows of life continually stir him up. His life is murky, unclear and full of dirt and trash.

To further compound his problem, the hopeless, ungodly man has no chance of acceptance by God or by God's people. In verse 5 David says that when he stands before God, the ungodly man will not be able to give any defense for his life or activities; neither will he be able to give even one reason why he should be permitted into God's presence.

Matthew 25 records some statements of the Lord Jesus Christ concerning His return to the earth to establish the millennial Kingdom. When the nations of the earth are gathered before Him, He will separate them as a shepherd separates sheep from goats. At that time He will say to the sheep, "Enter thou into the joy of thy lord" (vv. 21, 23). But he will say to the goats, "Depart from me, ye cursed, into everlasting fire . . ." (v. 41). At that judgment, as well as the judgment of the Great White Throne (Rev. 20:11-15), the unbeliever will have no recourse. All of his defenses and excuses will evaporate, and he will be denied access to the presence of God and the righteous.

The final destiny of the ungodly is to perish in eternal torment in the Lake of Fire, where prayers go unanswered, repentance brings no forgiveness and punishment produces no cleansing.

If you have not trusted the Lord Jesus Christ as your Savior, you are a hopeless man. Only when you receive the Savior will you possess life and hope and be named among the happy, blessed children of God. Do not delay. Trust Jesus Christ today.

What Is Your Answer?

1. What words does the psalmist use in verses 1 and 4 to identify two different kinds of men?

2. In what does the blessed man delight? How much time does he spend in meditation upon it? Do you think this should be true of a blessed man in our day?

3. What are four characteristics of the tree in verse 3? How would you relate them to the life of the blessed man?

4. According to verse 1, what three things does the blessed man *not* do?

5. According to verse 4, of what value is the ungodly man?

6. What prospect does the ungodly man have for being accepted by God or godly people?

7. What is the final destiny of the ungodly man?

CHAPTER 2

Give God the Glory

BIBLE PORTION TO READ: Psalm 8

IN SOME WAYS man and God are very much
alike. In other ways they are poles apart. When we
compare the extent of their abilities, the contrasts
are vast. Man is limited to one small place, while
God dwells beyond the starry heavens, walks the
vast mountain ranges of the universe, and even
abides within the heart of a man. Finite man
strains to stretch his limited comprehension of his
universe, but God knows all without reservation
or limitation.

Man strives to extend his brief life span by regu-
lating his diet, exercise and medical knowledge,
but he seldom passes the century mark. By contrast, God is eternal. His life knows no beginning,
no termination or so much as a pause. From its
beginning to its end, time is only a brief stroke of
the brush upon God's canvas of eternity.

Psalm 8 demonstrates that God has a glorious,
supreme position and that man, while less glorious than God, is the highest in order of all the
created beings.

17

The Excellent Name of God

More than one hundred years ago, the songwriter wrote:

> I know of Name, A beautiful Name,
> That angels brought down to earth;
> They whispered it low, One night long ago,
> To a maiden of lowly birth.

The chorus of the song concludes, "That matchless Name is Jesus." Many of us have fallen in love with the name Jesus, but we have neglected God's own personal name, Jehovah. In the Old Testament when the word LORD is spelled with capital letters, it is a translation of God's personal name, Jehovah.

We should never forget His name. It should be revered above all names. The third commandment says, "Thou shalt not take the name of the LORD thy God in vain; for the LORD will not hold him guiltless that taketh his name in vain" (Exod. 20:7). The Jews so honored the name of Jehovah that they would not even speak His name lest they take it in vain.

The name Jehovah comes from the Hebrew verb "to be." Exodus 3 records Jehovah's call and command to Moses to lead the Israelites from their bondage into the Promised Land. After some discussion with the Lord, Moses asked a question:

> Behold, when I come unto the children of
> Israel, and shall say unto them, The God of your
> fathers hath sent me unto you; and they shall say

Man's moral nature, his spiritual capabilities, his creative genius . . . and his emotional characteristics are all products of his creation in God's image.

A Verse to Memorize

"O LORD our Lord, how excellent is thy name in all the earth!" (Psalm 8:9).

to me, What is his name? what shall I say unto them?

And God said unto Moses, I AM THAT I AM: and he said, Thus shalt thou say unto the children of Israel, I AM hath sent me unto you (Exod. 3:13, 14).

Jehovah is the eternal, ever-present God. He is the I AM. The introduction and conclusion of Psalm 8 say that His name is excellent in all the earth.

To prove to Moses that He is Who He claimed to be, God asked Moses to throw his staff on the ground. When he did, the staff became a serpent. As Moses grabbed the serpent by the tail, it once again became his staff. God further confirmed His name by changing Moses' hand to a leprous white and then returning it again to its normal color. Thus God established the nature and character of His name with Moses by demonstrating His power over His creation.

Jehovah is not a God made of sticks and stones. He is the living God with a name that is appropriate for Him.

God's Exalted Glory

Besides having a great name, God has glory that exceeds that of any creature. When Paul met the Lord on the Damascus Road (Acts 9:3), he saw a light brighter than the noonday sun, a glory greater than the glory of the heavens.

Several years ago a group of young people sat on the front lawn of their home, waiting for an

19

eclipse of the sun. As the eclipse began, they watched the shadow begin to creep across the face of the sun. They were nearly blinded by the light of the sun, but they continued to watch for several minutes. The result was that all of them experienced damage to their eyes.

As harsh as the sun is to the naked eye, it is nothing compared with the glory of God. People in Moses' day were *afraid* that God would speak with them face to face. They believed that to look upon the face of God was certain death. His glory is higher than the heavens, brighter than the sun and more beautiful than any of the morning stars. All of the heavens declare the glory of God (Ps. 19:1).

God's Elemental Defense

Psalm 8:2 tells us that out of the mouths of babes God has ordained a strength that will quiet His enemies. In a recent worship service, the choir sang with perfect tone and enunciation. The words and music of the anthem were superior. But when the music ended, there were no hearty amens or praises to God. A few moments later the children's choir paraded to the platform to sing a children's song of praise about Daniel in the lions' den. Their voices were immature, and the words were occasionally jumbled, but their confidence in God and commitment to Him rang clearly through the auditorium. When they finished singing, hundreds of voices joined together in praising God.

That children's choir confirmed this verse of Scripture. God does not require the voice of mighty orators, the thunder of the heavens nor the power of a prince to defend Him. Rather, He chooses the voice of infants. When God approached Elijah to speak with Him, He did not come in the whirlwind or in the thunder. He spoke with a still, small voice.

Even in the days of our Lord Jesus Christ, little children were instruments of praise. In Matthew 21:15 and 16 the enemies of our Lord were angered by the wonderful things the children said in the temple. Other voices could have defended the honor and name of Jesus Christ, but He was contented with the utterances of children. Every utterance of theirs is apparently understood as constituting a part of the defense of God.

Every mother and father reading these words should remember that there is not a better word of praise that ever comes to your ears than praise from the mouth of a little child. The psalmist was right when he said, "Out of the mouth of babes and sucklings hast thou ordained strength [perfected praise]. . . ." God does not need your eloquence or brilliance to express His honor. Children do that best.

21

Man's Relation to the Universe

The observation of nature caused Charles Darwin to conclude that man was a culmination of the evolutionary process. Since that day, humanistic rationalism has compiled data intended to somehow relate man to his environment quite apart from any creative act of God. Spontaneous generation and the evolutionary theory disregard man in his proper place as a created being.

The psalmist was not troubled by such reasoning. He understood that God was the Creator of all things. However, as David observed the universe, he was confronted with an entirely different problem (v. 3). As he cared for his sheep on a cloudless night, the psalmist gazed into the starry heavens with amazement. Knowing that man was a mere speck on the face of the earth and that the earth was a small part of the universe, he could not comprehend how a God so vast and great could be interested in mankind. How could a God able to scatter thousands of stars with a single movement of His finger also be involved in the most minute details of a single, small creature lying on a lonely hillside in the dark of the night?

The psalmist spoke of the heavens as being the work of the fingers of God. Usually we do fine work with our fingers and heavy work with our hands. The gardener spades his garden with his hands, but a woman embroiders with her fingers. As he observed the heavens, David somehow thought of them as being the fine work of the fingers of God. This made it more difficult for him to perceive how God could actually be interested in a man. It prompted him to ask the question, "What is man, that thou art mindful of him?"

Some months ago I sat with a group of fishermen on a small island near Hudson Bay. We were a hundred miles from any civilization. Bear, moose and other wild animals were occasional visitors near our camp. There was little sign of civilization except an occasional airplane flying high in the sky, headed toward the North Pole.

As we sat musing around the fire, one man observed that, though we were far from civilization, we had nothing to worry about because several times a day planes followed the vector that took them directly overhead. As the conversation continued, however, we determined that even though the planes were flying over us at 39,000 feet, it would be impossible for us to attract their attention. Even if we could, they could not stop to assist us. They were simply too far up in the air and moving too fast to take any notice of us. David must have felt the same way as he thought about the God Who created the heavens. How could He possibly give any attention to a man?

Man's Rank in the Created Order

In answer to his own question, the psalmist declared why God looks upon man favorably and takes notice of him (v. 5). It is not because of man's significant size or strength. It is not because man populates a significant part of the earth or is particularly beautiful in his appearance. It is because God made man a little lower than Himself. Man is the epitome of God's earthbound creation. After God had created all of the other creatures, He concluded that He should make man in His own image. No other creature was given that honor.

Man's moral nature, his spiritual capabilities, his creative genius, his organizational strength, his determinative qualities, his desire for dominion and his emotional characteristics are all products of his creation in God's image. Consequently, man is very significant to God. In the order of created beings, only the angels, who have access to the presence of God and to the earth, stand supreme above him.

Man's Royal Crown

The psalmist declared that man wears a crown of glory, a diadem which signifies dignity and splendor. Man was created to have a special dignity. He walks with an upright bearing, clothes himself with beautiful attire, lives in beautifully decorated homes, and carefully maintains his gardens and lawns. He has a special glory all his own that is supreme above that of any other creatures of earth. It was his privilege to name the animals, have dominion over them and utilize them for his own purposes.

Man's Rule over Creation

The last thing the psalmist mentioned in relation to man's provision of glory is that he is dominant over all of the animals of creation (v. 6). The entire creation is man's dominion. Though man is insignificant in relation to the size of the universe, he is very significant as a special creation of God. He has special ability, dignity and dominion.

The writer of Hebrews recalled Psalm 8:5 in connection with the Lord Jesus Christ, declaring, "We see Jesus, who was made a little lower than the angels for the suffering of death . . ." (Heb. 2:9). In God's all-wise plan He chose to send the Lord Jesus Christ to earth as a man. It was only by becoming a man that He was able to bear the sins of men.

The death of the God-Man is our only way of deliverance from the condemnation of sin. The writer of Hebrews asked, "How shall we escape, if we neglect so great salvation . . ." (Heb. 2:3). The answer is obvious: There is no escape. Jesus

Christ's death is the only provision for salvation. As God the Son He suffered the penalty of sin and is now seated at the right hand of the Father, offering salvation to each one who will reach out to Him by faith.

What Is Your Answer?

1. What two sentences in Psalm 8 are identical? What significance do you think their location in the psalm has?

2. Compare Psalm 8:2; Matthew 21:15 and 16 and 1 Corinthians 1:26-29. What common teaching is found in these passages? What lessons may we learn from them?

3. What questions came to the psalmist's mind as he looked into the starry heavens?

4. According to verse 5, what is man's rank in the order of created beings?

5. In verse 6 how many of the works of God's hands are said to be under the dominion of man?

6. List five things included under man's dominion in verses 7 and 8.

7. With what is man crowned? What do you think this means?

CHAPTER 3

At Home with God

BIBLE PORTION TO READ: Psalm 15

IN RECENT YEARS our society has become
characterized by sarcasm, destruction, gossip,
lethargy and self-centeredness of astounding pro-
portions. Increasing numbers of husbands and
fathers desert their homes. Wives are leaving their
God-given roles to seek their place in the sun.
Children are in rebellion against their parents and
authority in general. Vast numbers of people have
lost their sense of responsibility to keep commitments or give an honest day's work.

The conditions have prevailed in other generations. But in our generation they have worked
their way into the fiber of even fundamental
churches across the land. Pastors report rebellious
children, broken homes, promiscuity, abusive
slander and general carnality on every hand. Our
churches are faltering in their attempt to evange-
lize a lost and perishing world because they are
weakened by selfish, personal sins from within.

Christians should not be characterized by such
dark and unwholesome things. Surely if they walk

with God and are planning to spend eternity with Him in Heaven, they should live faithful, loving, kind and unselfish lives. James 3:13 and 17 ask a question and issue an appropriate challenge:

> Who is a wise man and endued with knowledge among you? let him shew out of a good conversation his works with meekness of wisdom. . . .
> But the wisdom that is from above is first pure, then peaceable, gentle, and easy to be intreated, full of mercy and good fruits, without partiality, and without hypocrisy.

The Questions

Many years ago David addressed himself to a similar question and answered it with a list of characteristics that describe a man of God. The two questions in Psalm 15:1 are addressed personally to Jehovah. We know this is a rhetorical question because David proceeded to give the answer himself and did not wait for an answer from God. We must understand, however, that his answer is the answer that God would have given—not the answer of a rationalistic, humanistic thinker.

The first question asks for a description of the man who walks along with God every day of his life. The second question reveals an interest in knowing what kind of a man will live with God forever in Heaven. These are significant questions in a day when standards of conduct are lowered so far that it is difficult to distinguish Christians from non-Christians in a godless society. Every one of us needs to face these questions squarely. If a man is walking with God, how does he behave? And if he is going to spend his eternity in Heaven with God, what things should characterize his life? The psalmist identified three general charac-

A Verse to Memorize

"LORD, who shall abide in thy tabernacle? who shall dwell in thy holy hill?" (Psalm 15:1).

teristics of this kind of person in the second verse of Psalm 15.

He Lives Uprightly

To walk uprightly (v. 2a) means to live a life that is complete and without blemish. This life is full and well balanced. It accomplishes all of the things intended for it. This kind of life is not marred by great personal sins or destructive forces that discredit otherwise usable spiritual gifts. The upright life is unlike the lives of the Pharisees of Jesus' day who appeared as sepulchres painted white on the outside yet were tainted with the stench of dead men within.

He Works Righteously

The person who walks with God and will spend eternity in Heaven also meets the standards of God in all of his behavior. Righteousness is legislative holiness. When a man works righteousness, his activities conform to the holy standards of God. He does not practice compromise or libertinism.

Three high schoolers were standing in the hall outside their Sunday School classroom recently, talking about their activities of the night before. One had attended a beach party with a dozen unbelieving friends from school. The other two were describing their behavior with their boy-friends in the family room of one of their homes. As I listened to them, I wondered if they walked with God. It seemed apparent to me that they did not. I also wondered if they were on their way to Heaven. Righteousness did not characterize their lives.

He Speaks Honestly

> O, what a tangled web we weave
> When first we practice to deceive.

The life of a genuine man of God is lived in such a way that he does not have to live or speak a lie. He can be trusted by his friends because he tells the truth.

Having named the qualities of uprightness, righteousness and honesty, David moved on to talk about specific things that are found in the life of the man who journeys with God. He listed eight specific things in verses 2-5. Six of them are negative; only two are positive, but they paint a vivid picture for us. Our consideration of them enables us to recognize this kind of person in the midst of a distorted generation.

He Does Not Slander

The word *backbite* (v. 3) means "to slander." A slanderer looks for information, true or untrue, about an individual and then repeats it in such a way as to injure him. Any little tidbit taken out of its context, expanded and embellished with inflections of the voice or innuendo is capable of disheartening the guilty person and destroying the innocent.

Little people use this device to make themselves look big while they destroy a large opponent. Selfish people get gain for themselves while they rob a richer neighbor. The slothful appears more precise while he drags his hardworking companion into disrepute. A pauper seems to glitter as he

Daily Bible Readings

Sunday—Fellowship in God's House—
   Hebrews 10:19-25
Monday—Forever with God—Revelation
   21:1-8
Tuesday—Better to Obey—1 Samuel
   15:17-26
Wednesday—Consecrated Conversation—
   Ephesians 4:29—5:4
Thursday—Practice What You Preach—
   Matthew 23:13-31
Friday—Slaughtered by Slander—Proverbs
   26:17-22
Saturday—Honoring the Proper People—
   Romans 13:1-7

smears mud on the garments of his prestigious
cousin. Slander infects every walk of life. It serves
as a cutting device by which a malicious person
destroys another through derogatory comments
based upon fact or fiction. Slander has no place in
the church. It is better to stand in silence than
slander a saint.

He Does Not Destroy

The man who walks with God will not do evil
to people whom he meets in his daily routine (v.
3b). The word *evil* means "suffering misfortune or
destruction." A man who walks with God does not
wish to cause people suffering or misfortune.

Our society is filled with people who delight in
the destruction of their friends or foes, laugh at the
losses of individuals or companies and rejoice in
the rejection of public figures great and small.
Some are so sadistic as to gain gratification from
pain inflicted upon others. While none of us

would desire to be a sadist, there are many who do gain some satisfaction out of another's misfortunes.

God is kind and tenderhearted. He has provided redemption. Because He is not willing that any should perish, He sent the Savior to seek and to save that which was lost. When we walk with God, we take on the same characteristics. One of the characteristics of the reign of Jesus Christ on earth is that men will no longer inflict agony and pain upon others. "They shall not hurt nor destroy in all my holy mountain: for the earth shall be full of the knowledge of the LORD, as the waters cover the sea" (Isa. 11:9). When Jesus Christ returns to the earth to establish the millennial Kingdom, He will judge the destroyers of earth and lead men to live in harmony with one another.

He Does Not Ridicule

Sarcasm is a multimillion dollar business as well as the pastime of people rich and poor. Many people create humor at someone else's expense. They laugh at the fallen drunk who is trying to right himself at the curb while he utters oaths with slurred speech. They imitate the person who stutters or limps and tell derogatory jokes with great delight and satisfaction.

God does not engage in sarcasm for purposes of destruction or pleasure. His children should refrain from those things also. It is a shame for pastors, youth workers, Sunday School teachers or people in the pew to use this tool of the unsaved man.

He Despises Worthless People

God evaluates people well (v. 4a). He does not place any laurels on the wicked, nor does He put crowns on the reprobate. He does not lift up the worthless or immoral, nor does He reward the workers of iniquity with grace and glory. Only Satan's hosts and wicked men do that. They venerate the vile and not the venerable. The social and entertainment worlds are filled with idols who are often the worst reprobates in our society.

A man who lives his life in the presence of God and the expectation of Glory is the person who is filled with disdain and disgust when he sees the reprobate. All of the prophets of the Old Testament preached against unrighteousness and condemned ungodliness. They evaluated the worth of a person by his relationship to Jehovah. John the Baptist and Jesus Christ did the same and pronounced heavy condemnation upon those who lived in sin.

He Honors Godly People

If a man honors another, he gives him the weight of his attention and the power of his influence (v. 4b). A famous missionary statesman recently recalled speaking to a group of young people in a well-known Baptist church in the Midwest. During his message the young people carried on casual conversations with one another, wrote notes, laughed out loud at inappropriate times and refused to bow their heads for an invitation.

As he repeated the story, he was visibly shaken to the point of tears. He had endeavored to tell them a great story of missions, the faithfulness of God, the salvation of souls and the building of churches, but the teens had refused to honor him by giving him their attention. God Himself honors a righteous man and upholds him with the right arm of His strength. Any man, woman or child who treads through life arm in arm with God will also honor those who fear the Lord.

He Keeps His Commitments

It is one thing to make a commitment; it is quite another to keep it (v. 4c). People make all kinds of commitments they do not keep. Oftentimes they will turn and walk away from a promise or vow without any second thought.

This seems to be a special characteristic of the generation in which we live. One person reasons, "I got in a little bit over my head, so I think I'll go bankrupt and forget it." Another will say, "I married a lousy husband, so I think I'll divorce him and see if I can find myself a decent one." A young person will say, "I know I was supposed to be home at 11:00 and I told you I would, but something came up." People are no longer willing to stand by a promise if it is not convenient.

A godly person, whether old or young, will stand behind his vows, even if it is detrimental to himself. A bad deal made in a rash moment is binding upon the person who has God's perspective. His word is as good as his bond. He performs his oaths without modification or rebate, even though they may prove to be to his own disadvantage. He will arrive when he is supposed to arrive to do what he is supposed to do in the manner in which he is to do it. That is a characteristic of those who will be in Heaven.

He Does Not Take Financial Advantage

A shrewd businessman was eating lunch with some of his friends. He laughed over a deal he had just consummated. He had received a large down payment on a piece of property with very large monthly payments. He was satisfied that the individual who had purchased the property would not be able to make the payments. Foreclosure would bring the property back to the seller and permit him to keep the large down payment as well. The businessman was taking unfair advantage of the buyer.

Often usury fell into this same category in the Old Testament. The law of Moses prohibited charging usury from an Israelite, especially if he was poor or in need. While lenders could collect usury from strangers, they were not allowed to oppress the brethren with such things. In the same way, a man of God will not take advantage of others by placing them in an impossible financial situation or charging exorbitant rates of interest (v. 5a).

He Does Not Accept Bribes

The last thing David said in this psalm about the man who walks with God is that he does not accept a reward against an innocent person (v. 5b). The bribery of judges or persons in responsible positions was common in Old Testament days just as it is today. But a godly man will neither be involved in giving nor receiving such tainted money.

It would be a good exercise for a believer to list the eight characteristics from these verses on a note card and carry it until he learns to practice them every day. May God grant you a fresh commitment to live a life characterized by these traits.

What Is Your Answer?

1. What important question is asked in Psalm 15:1? What do you think this means for believers today?

2. What three activities are mentioned in Psalm 15:2?

3. What do you think it means for a man to speak truth in his heart?

4. What two things does this man not do to his neighbor, according to verse 3?

5. Does verse 4 teach that this man will always have positive thoughts about everyone?

6. What three characteristics in verses 4 and 5 indicate that this man is unselfish?

CHAPTER 4

Confidence and Crying

BIBLE PORTION TO READ: Psalm 27

CAN CONFIDENCE and crying exist in the same person at the same time? At first thought this combination may seem impossible. But after further consideration, it becomes apparent that crying (pleading) is often based upon confidence.

In Psalm 27 David expressed great confidence in God. The first six verses of the psalm express this great trust. In the last six verses David cried out to God with a pleading prayer. Confidence was the foundation upon which he built his prayer life. Because of God's past care for the king, David knew God would hear and answer his prayer for the problems he faced day by day. David's confidence had an extraordinary effect upon him.

Confidence Quiets Fear

Having declared that Jehovah was his light and his salvation, David asked the question, "Whom shall I fear?" the obvious answer is, no one. His God provided light in his life. Therefore, David was unafraid of the sin around him.

Many people are afraid of the dark where unseen and unknown things lurk. The same things viewed in the light of day produce no fear whatsoever.

Debbie Lynn was a very happy little girl, a genuine pleasure to her parents. One evening after she was put to bed, she became restless and began to scream. Her mother went to the room and picked her up. When the little girl had quieted down, she put her back in bed; but as she left the room, Debbie began to scream once again. Night after night this problem continued without relief.

The worried mother urged her husband to do something about the situation. So he went into his daughter's room and sat down beside the bed while the mother turned out the light and left. Suddenly he saw something he had not noticed before. A streetlight down the block was shining through the branches of the trees just outside the window. It cast shadows on the wall at the foot of the bed. As the wind blew gently, the branches seemed to reach down toward the bed with grotesquely shaped fingers.

Debbie began to scream. Her father's first impulse was to scream with her. But understanding that the grasping hands were only shadows on the wall, he got up from his place beside the bed and turned on a little light. With a flick of the switch, the terrible shadows of the darkness were gone, and the little girl's fears were stilled. Debbie slept peacefully thereafter because she had nothing

---

When the Christian's life becomes so filled with activities, involvements and investments that he cannot see clearly, he is often attacked and defeated by his enemies. . . .

---

to fear. The imagined foes of darkness were removed.

All of us have been afraid of the darkness of the world about us. We have cried to the Lord, and He has come to dispel the darkness and wondering. The confusion and stumbling caused by sin have been taken away and confidence has been restored. The Lord has become our light even as He was David's light.

David also declared that the Lord was his salvation and the strength of his life. Time after time God miraculously delivered the psalmist and gave him strength to live his life as he faced wild animals and the willful men of his day. As the strength of David's life, God stepped in to become a shield, a wall and hedge when David was in desperate need of protection.

Confidence Conquers Foes

David did not play the peer group game. He was able to stand alone (v. 2). It did not matter to him one whit if an entire host encamped against him. He knew that if the odds were a thousand to one, everything was going to be all right because God would defeat his enemies.

Can you imagine a solitary figure facing an entire army in a battle? The desperation of such a situation would drive that lone soldier to flight or despair unless he knew that an almighty force was on his side to defeat the foe.

When I was a very small child, my nights were occasionally disturbed by a recurring nightmare. In my dream everybody in school was against me. My brothers, who usually protected me, were not nearby to help. The other students would endeavor to beat me or throw desks at me, but somehow they could never actually get to me. There always seemed to be an invisible field between me and the opponents into which they were throwing themselves only to be rebuffed or injured.

David knew that God had served as that invisible shield so that when his enemies approached him, they stumbled and fell. Their greatest efforts were not enough to come near the man of God.

Confidence Gives Calm

David explained that in the midst of the tumult coming against him, he had no fear (v. 3). His confidence in the Lord gave him great quietness in his heart.

The expectation of doom troubles the timid mind and produces a pounding heart in the mature believer. The anticipation of problems causes the Christian to be silent when he should speak and to retreat when he should fight. With trembling hands, he freezes in terror, waiting for the worst.

But great men of faith had a confidence in God that would not allow them to falter in the face of great odds. They were filled with a powerful calm that took them from battle to battle, through clashing swords and prancing hooves to victory for God.

Confidence Prompts Fellowship, Prayer, Praise

A desperate, fearful person has a tendency to be very self-centered. He is worried about what is

Daily Bible Readings

Sunday—The Lord, the Light—John 1:1-9
Monday—Men Love Darkness—John 3:17-21
Tuesday—Called into Light—1 Peter 2:9, 10
Wednesday—No Cause for Fear— 1 Samuel 17:31-37, 45-47
Thursday—Exchange Peace for Anxiety— Philippians 4:6, 7
Friday—Singlemindedness—James 1:1-8
Saturday—Boldness with God—Hebrews 4:14-16

going to happen to him. He needs continual reassurance. Well-defined objectives give way to simple self-preservation. Preoccupation with problems inhibits ambition and saps strength. Movement gives way to lethargy, and accomplishment is swallowed up by defeat.

The man who has great confidence in God, however, takes certain well-defined steps that produce happy results (vv. 4-6). In verse 4 David said he would seek the house of God and behold the beauty of the Lord all the days of his life. He would also go to the temple for prayer. The confident man of God will be victorious over his enemies and will create sacrifices of joy through song and praises to the Lord.

It is inappropriate to have undue confidence in ourselves in the humanistic sense, but it is appropriate to have confidence in God, knowing full well that with God on our side, we can be more than conquerors. We can look at the future with expectation and plan for accomplishments in the name of God, realizing that the One Who has begun a good work will perform it until the day of Jesus Christ (Phil. 1:6).

Having stated this confidence, David turned to prayer. Six specific requests came from his lips as he cried out to Jehovah.

A Cry for the Attention of God

Several years ago the newspapers carried an article about a woman who poisoned her husband's coffee while he sat in the family room, reading the evening paper. During the trial she confessed that she was angry because he never listened to her when she talked to him. Arriving home from work, he would hide himself in the family room and read the paper to the neglect of his wife. She related that as she walked into the family room carrying his coffee, she told him very clearly that the coffee was poisoned. He replied, "Thank you," and drank it anyway.

Each of us at some time has spoken to another person who did not listen. At times even God does not give ear to the cries of men. Isaiah said, "Your iniquities have separated between you and your God, and your sins have hid his face from you, that he will not hear" (Isa. 59:2).

The child of God is to plead for the attention of God. When Elijah faced the prophets of Baal on Mount Carmel, he pleaded for the ear of Jehovah: "Hear me, O LORD, hear me, that this people may know that thou art the LORD God, and that thou hast turned their heart back again" (1 Kings 18:37). Calling for the attention of God demonstrates our intensity and sincerity of heart as God's children.

David was responding to God's command by seeking His face (v. 8). His very first desire was that the God in Whom he trusted would grant him full attention for the problems that confronted him.

A Cry for the Assistance of God

Four strong phrases in verse 9 indicate David's intense desire for God's assistance in his life. The first, "Hide not thy face far from me," involves God's watch care. When a pilot flies his plane into heavy clouds, he wants to know that an observer at some radar screen knows his location and the location of other planes in the vicinity. Without the watchful eye of the radar observer, he might collide with another plane.

In a similar way, David requested God to keep His eye constantly on him to guide and guard him along the course of his life.

His second plea was that God not put him away or isolate him because of failure or sin in his life. His third request was a plea that God not be preoccupied temporarily to the neglect of David. Like a little child being left in the nursery at church, David cried out, "Leave me not."

His fourth request was that God not forsake him. David had no desire to be left to his own devices. He was dependent upon God and knew that no amount of his own knowledge or prowess could preserve him.

A Cry for the Attachment of God

The psalmist said, "When my father and my mother forsake me, then the LORD will take me up" (v. 10). Family loyalty and protection are among the most precious possessions on earth. But with the rising incidence of working mothers, absentee fathers, divorce and outside entertainment, children are often left to themselves. They languish in neglect or seek the companionship and advice of peers who lead them astray. The Lord Jesus Christ informed His disciples that they must be willing to forsake father and mother in order to follow Him (Matt. 10:36, 37). David needed and expected God to be attached to him even though his family should forsake him.

A Cry for the Advice of God

Every child of God needs to let God chart the course of his life lest he become confused by the storms and cross-currents of his environment (v. 11a). Desperation rises in the heart of a man lost in the forest without a compass, adrift on a sea without charts or wandering in the darkness without light.

God has graciously given us a chart and compass. It is His holy Word. In it He gives advice for any situation in life. David himself could say, "Thy word is a lamp unto my feet, and a light unto my path" (Ps. 119:105). Besides the infallible Guidebook, God has given to every believer a personal Interpreter and Guide Who is the Holy Spirit. Because God has given a written and a personal Guide, every believer may sing with great confidence:

> Guide me, O Thou great Jehovah,
> Pilgrim thru this barren land;
> I am weak, but Thou art mighty—
> Hold me with Thy pow'rful hand.

A Cry for an Uncluttered Life

David was concerned that he be spared from paths strewn with trees, brush and rocks because his enemies often lurked along the path to destroy him (v. 11b). He wanted an open road down which he could walk where no enemy could attack him by surprise. He wanted God to keep his life free from the clutter that harbored desperate foes of his life.

Every believer should pray that prayer. When

the Christian's life becomes so filled with activities, involvements and investments that he cannot see clearly, he is often attacked and defeated by his enemies—whether they be men or demons. Single-minded simplicity furnishes a safe walkway for the child of God.

A Cry for an Undefeated Life

David's final cry was for survival and success under the sovereign hand of God. David anticipated success because he was confident, but cried to God nevertheless for his continued preservation in the midst of a hostile world (v. 12).

Having expressed his confidence and his cry, David concluded with verse 14: "Wait on the LORD: be of good courage, and he shall strengthen thine heart: wait, I say, on the LORD." We should walk in His way, witness to the world and wait upon the Lord.

What Is Your Answer?

1. What emotion is the subject of the two questions of verse 1? Is this emotion a good or a bad emotion?

2. What was David's attitude in verse 3 in the face of war and evil men who sought to destroy him?

3. Verse 4 tells us that David desired one thing of the Lord. What was it, and what did it mean?

4. What kind of sacrifice did David desire to offer to God (v. 6)?

5. To whom should a child of God turn when his father and mother forsake him?

6. What do you think David meant by "a plain path" in verse 11? Why did he desire it?

7. What must the believer do if he wants to be strengthened by God?

44

CHAPTER 5

A Sinner's Prayer

BIBLE PORTION TO READ: Psalm 51:1-11

ONE OF GOD'S greatest servants walked on the roof of his home in the late afternoon of a beautiful Middle Eastern day. He contemplated the great plan God had arranged for his life. A vast kingdom had been delivered into his hands. Through military prowess and the protection of God he had been granted victory over his enemies. God had truly blessed his life with success.

He must have recalled his battles with bears and giants as well as the armies of the nations all about him. As the second king of the nation of Israel, he was enjoying a success story unequalled by the kings from nearby nations. Even while he walked on the roof that evening, his armies were engaged in victorious battles against enemies who dared to stand against the great warrior and his God.

As he looked from the roof of his palatial home, his eyes came to rest upon a woman who was bathing herself, perhaps in a courtyard or on a roof nearby. She was very beautiful.

This brief account begins the story of David's great sin with Bath-sheba, the murder of Uriah her husband and the death of an illegitimate child. David's sin led him into darkness, despair, disgrace and defeat. When he was confronted by the prophet Nathan, who condemned him as the stealer of a woman and the murderer of an innocent man, David's spirit was crushed within him. Guilt was piled upon guilt in his broken heart.

In the hours that followed, David sat at his table and penned his words of repentance. As was his custom, David wrote those words in the form of a song. They have been recorded as Psalm 51. The first eleven verses contain prayers—a prayer of repentance in verses 1-9 and a prayer of renewal in verses 10 and 11.

Great sin always calls for repentance and renewal. These two things must happen in their proper order. When sin has been committed, it is always necessary that repentance be the first step in restoring the sinner to a place of usefulness in the will of God. After repentance has worked its course, renewal must take place before productivity can be restored. In this psalm David followed the proper order for restoration and ministry.

A Prayer of Repentance

David's prayer of repentance involves six separate items, each of which should come from a truly repentant heart.

A cry for mercy. Grace is a characteristic of

Grace is a characteristic of God that allows Him to give sinful men things they do not deserve. His mercy, on the other hand, is a characteristic that causes Him to withhold punishment from an individual who deserves it.

God that allows Him to give to sinful men things they do not deserve. His mercy, on the other hand, is a characteristic that causes Him to withhold punishment from an individual who deserves it. David pleaded that God would withhold from him the wrath he should have received because of the chain of sins he had forged.

No man should ever want what he deserves from God because every man deserves death and hell as a result of his sin. Only the mercy of God withholds the hand of God's violence upon rebellious and sin-distorted mankind.

Several years ago a psychological consultant from Wichita, Kansas, told the Utah Association for Mental Health that parental spankings promote the notion that violence against others is legitimate. He said that spanking was the first half-inch on the yardstick of violence and that it was followed by hitting, and ultimately by rape, murder and assassination.

Students of the Bible remember what the writer of the Proverbs said: "Foolishness is bound in the heart of a child; but the rod of correction shall drive it far from him" (Prov. 22:15). Like earthly parents, God also punishes those who act foolishly. The repentant person, knowing what he deserves, must cry out to God for mercy, recognizing that his behavior will bring the wrath of God unless mercy is extended to him.

David asked God to measure his mercy by his own loving-kindness. The word *loving-kindness* suggests the loyalty of one individual to another because of an established love relationship that is accompanied by an agreement, perhaps even a covenant. God had certainly expressed his loving-kindness toward David, and David pleaded for mercy on the basis of a past covenant relationship.

Often there are occasions in a marriage when a husband or a wife will plead for mercy and forgiveness on the basis of a covenant made at an altar when they were united in marriage.

When company is coming and the wife has cleaning to do, food to prepare and dishes to wash, she appreciates having her husband come home immediately after work. When he decides instead to leave work two hours early to play golf and finally arrives home a half hour before dinner, bragging about his golf score, his wife will undoubtedly be upset. Her feelings are justified, but she does not dismiss him nor divorce him because of that.

Because of the rich love that brought about their marriage, she will forgive and seek to be restored to the kind of fellowship they had enjoyed before. This happens, of course, when the husband realizes what he has done, confesses his failure to his wife and asks for the extension of her mercy, resulting in his forgiveness and restoration.

A plea for clearing of the record. When a child does something wrong, his parent has the option either to forgive and forget or to punish him. In the spring after my tenth birthday, I put a rock in my sling shot, took careful aim and released the rock in the general direction of an obnoxious sparrow. But without thinking, I had inadvertently aimed the rock at the kitchen window of our farm home.

As the window shattered, I knew I had commit-

ted a sin. My mother had told me many times never
to shoot rocks toward the house. I had done it,
however, and the evidence was clearly visible.
When I saw what had happened, I ran out of the
yard past the barn and down the lane toward the
garden where my mother was working. I crossed
the creek and climbed up the big bank, sobbing
every inch of the way.

When my mother saw me crying, she assumed I
was hurt. She came over, put her arms around me
and asked what was the matter. I blurted out over
and over again, "I broke the kitchen window. I
broke the kitchen window." My mother did not
beat me. She did not criticize me. She simply
erased the debt of my act. I'll never forget that. She
reacted to me in tenderness.

David knew that his relationship with God had
been broken because of his sin. In tears he pleaded
for an erasing of the debt. God graciously blotted
it out so that he would need to plead no more.

A request for cleansing. "Wash me throughly

49

from mine iniquity, and cleanse me from my sin" (v. 2). Every genuinely repentant person desires complete cleansing and forsaking of his sin. He does not casually bow a knee before God and request that a portion of his sin be taken away and the rest retained. Nor does he ask for a temporary cleansing so he may go again into the streets when darkness comes to live in his sin once again.

David prayed for cleansing through and through. He could see the filth of his spiritual garments and wanted nothing more to do with them until they were absolutely clean. The dark, dirty colors of his sin did not match the expected righteousness of the king's life, so he begged for the scrubbing and pounding of God upon the rock of His cleansing at the river of forgiveness. David's request for cleansing was based upon a full recognition of wrongdoing on his part. He did not have a glib attitude toward the extent of his sin.

A recognition of sin. David fully acknowledged his transgression. As a matter of fact, his sin was so prominent in his mind that he said, "My sin is ever before me."

Medical treatment of leprosy has completely altered the position of the leper in society. There was a day when a leper could never forget that he had the dreaded disease. Community regulations required that he absent himself from commonly visited places. Whenever anyone walked down the road, the leper was required to get into the ditch. He could not stay on the road with travelers.

The leper could not pollute anyone. Until he could gain cleansing, he was separated from the community. Whenever anyone approached him on the path, he had to cry out, "Unclean, unclean, unclean," so the person would know a leper was close at hand. The leper's dreadful disease was always on his mind.

David was in the same position with his sin. It was always before him. Every place he turned he saw reminders of what he had done. Day and night the thoughts of his sin were raging through his troubled mind. In verse 4 David confessed that his sin was primarily against God. He was fully conscious that he had sinned against Bath-sheba and Uriah. But the Creator of heaven and earth had also been wronged, and David had to seek reconciliation with Him.

Every one of our sins is aimed directly at God. When little Herman Smith climbed over the fence into the neighbor's chicken yard and began to kill chickens, he was hurting the chickens. In a certain sense he was transgressing against them. But the major offense was against the farmer who owned the chickens, and that farmer prosecuted him.

When David sinned against Bath-sheba and Uriah, he did transgress against them, but he transgressed against their God in a greater way. David was very much aware that God would prosecute him. He needed the forgiveness of the Sovereign Whose children he had violated.

When we sin against one of God's children, we must remember to seek not only the forgiveness of the child of God, but also the forgiveness of God Himself because we have violated Him as well as His child.

A realization of depravity. Four little skunks followed their mother along the creek that flowed past an old farm home. As the family dog bounded off the porch to chase the trespassers from the edge of the creek, the mother skunk sprayed the little dog with her obnoxious protective spray. The little dog turned back toward the house to escape the distasteful experience.

The most amusing thing about that simple incident was the manner in which each of the little skunks also turned his back to the dog and raised his tail in defiance. The instinct to emit the foul odor of the skunk was present in the little ones even though they had not yet matured to a point where they could accomplish their nasty act.

David fully recognized the potential of his life when he said, "Behold, I was shapen in iniquity; and in sin did my mother conceive me" (v. 5). He knew that his propensity to sin had been present in him from his very earliest days. He was depraved by nature. His poor, repentant heart was aware of his great tendencies, and with a clear recognition of that, he cried out to God for a solution.

A plea for a solution. David's primary concern was that he might once again be able to hear joy and gladness so that his broken heart could sing. Depression overwhelmed him. He could not sleep; he could not eat. Apathy and lethargy were common feelings. He was often filled with anxiety, fear and hopelessness. He felt worthless, and tears often came upon him. His despair brought him to the place of repentance. Now the first progress beyond repentance began to manifest itself. He had a deep-seated desire once again to know joy and happiness.

A Prayer for Renewal

Modern wash-and-wear clothes have taken much of the drudgery out of the laundry process. In earlier days when housewives washed white shirts to remove the dirt, they also removed the starch from the collars. Before the husband could wear his shirt again, it was necessary to put the starch back into the collar and to press it carefully so it would retain its shape.

In the first part of David's prayer, he requested that the dirt be removed from him. In the next part of his prayer, he requested that he be "starched" once again in order to be useful to God. There is more to getting right with God than simply a confession of sin. There must also be the conscientious seeking of renewal.

The psalmist prayed for four specific things. The first is a clean heart (v. 10a). The second is a good or right spirit (v. 10b). The third is the abiding presence of God (v. 11a). And the fourth is the continued presence of the Holy Spirit of God, empowering him for service and ministry (v. 11b). These positive requests are summed up in the words of the songwriter:

> Jesus, fill now with Thy Spirit
> Hearts that full surrender know,
> That the streams of living water
> From our inner man may flow.

Repentance and renewal are the first two steps the believer should take if he falls into sin. They are the pathway that leads to usefulness and blessing. Without them, no amount of labor, compensation or self-recrimination can bring the believer into the will of God.

Is fellowship with Jesus Christ missing from your life? Are you living with unconfessed sin? Come to the Savior in repentance. Give Him your broken heart and ask for renewed fellowship once again. He will forgive, and the joy of walking with Jesus Christ will be restored.

What Is Your Answer?

1. What attributes of God do you see in this passage?

2. What attribute prompts God's mercy?

3. What had David done that qualified him for God's cleansing?

4. Why did David say his sin was only against God?

5. Why do you think David had such confidence that God would cleanse him?

6. Why do you suppose God had "broken" David's bones (v. 8)?

7. What was David's hope for protection against committing this sin again?

CHAPTER 6

Resolutions That Work

BIBLE PORTION TO READ: Psalm 51:12-19

AFTER HIS SIN with Bath-sheba and subsequent confrontation by Nathan, David crumbled in repentance under the crushing load of his guilt (2 Sam. 12; Ps. 51). In due time, repentance came with confession of his sin, a plea for mercy and restoration to fellowship with God. All of these things occurred in David's life, but they were not the end of the matter.

Something more needed to happen to the king of Israel. It was as though he was all dressed up with no place to go. He was like the fabled spinster of the Missouri hills who took her regular Saturday evening bath, dressed in her very best gown and sat on the porch all evening because she was never asked to a party.

Somewhere beyond repentance and renewal comes reinvolvement in the work of God. David's desire was to be deeply involved in the work of Jehovah. In order to put his desire into practice, he made four clear-cut resolutions that would thrust him back into a place of responsible activity. Genuine repentance will always include some resolutions that declare the restored sinner's intention to work for God once again.

From time to time since New Testament days, some Christians have developed a morbid attitude about life. They promote the crucifixion of self and the denial of pleasure. They live morosely in the shadow of the cross and the tomb. Some of this kind of thinking is profitable because it leads to confession and cleansing. But if it is dwelt upon too much to the neglect of the miracle of new life in Christ and joyful service for the King of Kings, it becomes an overwhelming burden.

Each believer is cleansed by the blood of Christ. For that reason he may lift his eyes toward Heaven with hope and anticipation of great service for God. The harvest fields are ripe. The Word must be taught. Disciples must be made. Families must be strengthened. Fellowship must be sweet, and songs should fill the air as the army of Christ marches to victory.

David understood this. Though his life had been marred by great sin, he repented and made resolutions. His list is not comprehensive, but it does demonstrate the kind of resolutions every believer should make when he is in similar circumstances.

You will notice that before David stated each resolution, he made a request. His resolutions are not based upon whim or human effort. They rest solidly upon the provision of God. Before he made any promise, he prayed for divine provision. When believers in our generation learn to follow

---

Genuine repentance will always include some resolutions that declare the restored sinner's intention to work for God once again.

---

this pattern, they will experience less disillusionment and greater success in carrying out their earnest resolves.

Resolution #1: Concerning Evangelism

David's first request and resolve concerned his witness to sinners. First and Second Samuel portray David as an outspoken man. He rebuked those who were walking contrary to the will of God. He taught them what their relationship with the Lord should be and what the consequences of disobedience were.

Sin silenced the voice of that great witness. He dared not speak to sinners about the waywardness of their lives because of his own sin. It is usually true that a man becomes soft toward other people's sins when he himself is living in sin.

In Matthew 16:21 Jesus Christ began to tell His disciples about His coming death. Peter rebuked the Lord and said He should not plan to die. Jesus spoke very sharply to His disciple, telling him that he did not savor the things that were of God but those that were of men. Then in verse 24 He said, "If any man will come after me, let him deny himself, and take up his cross, and follow me." Because Peter savored the things of men, he was not ready to follow the Lord Jesus Christ to Calvary.

His fleshly attitudes came to full light only a

few days later when he was confronted by the young woman in the court of Pilate's judgment hall. So intent was he upon self-preservation that he would not confess that he knew Jesus Christ. Worldly attitudes close the mouth of a witness. Like Peter, many a believer who has worldly attitudes finds his mouth completely stopped.

Before David made his resolution about witnessing, he requested that God restore to him the joy of his salvation and promised that he would be a witness when that joy returned.

The believer never feels like witnessing when he has experienced spiritual or moral defeat. When he knows that nothing has worked right for him, when God seems far off or when bitterness wells up within him, he does not feel like walking into the street to witness for the Savior. It is very difficult to admonish another person to be right with God when we are not right with God ourselves.

It is at that point that the sinning Christian needs to repent and ask God for the joy of forgiveness and deliverance so he may once again bear witness for Jesus Christ. David did not pray for the restoration of salvation. He prayed for the restoration of the *joy* of salvation.

He also asked God to uphold him with His free spirit. This is probably not the Holy Spirit of God, but a willing spirit. He needed the support of a willing spirit from God, a spirit willing to be used of God. Often when people have been involved in sin and return to the Lord, they declare they will never be a witness again. They sit back and remain silent, and their unwillingness to be involved only drives them into further isolation. David cried out to the Lord, asking for both joy and a willing spirit. He knew that when he received them, he would become an active witness once again.

Daily Bible Readings

Sunday—The Bearers of Glad Tidings—
Romans 10:8-17

Monday—A Prayer for Laborers—Matthew
9:35-38

Tuesday—The Preparation of a Witness—
Acts 9:17-22

Wednesday—A Call for Praise—Psalm
150

Thursday—Facing God's Righteous
Demands—Romans 3:21-26

Friday—A Song of Forgiveness—Psalm
30

Saturday—Our Adequate God—Psalm
145:8-21

Resolution #2: Concerning the Presentation of Righteousness

Before David made his resolution about righteousness, he presented a request to Jehovah for deliverance from bloodguiltiness. He certainly was guilty of the blood of Uriah the Hittite and other men. But the term *bloodguiltiness* has to do with the penalty of all sin that demands the death of the sinner. David had committed at least two sins that demanded his death. One of them was his adulterous relationship with Bath-sheba, and the other was the murder of Uriah.

David knew he must either be delivered from the penalty of his sins or suffer death in order that the righteous law of God be satisfied. Gary Gilmore demanded the death penalty when he was convicted for the crime of murder. His rationale for the demand was that he did not deserve to live. He reasoned that because of what he had done, he deserved to die. As a result, he was executed before

59

a firing squad, thus paying his final debt to society.

For God's law to be sustained, King David knew that he had to be punished as a lawbreaker. He could never again speak of God's righteousness or His righteous law unless God somehow balanced his account by removing his guilt. David's request preceded his promise to sing or shout about the righteousness of God once again. If God could take care of his problem, David would openly speak about God's righteous law and the necessity of obedience to it.

When Christians get involved in sin, it is amazing how their attitude toward God's righteous standards change. Suddenly they rationalize their behavior, justify things that are completely wrong and talk about how unfair God is or how unreasonable in His demands.

Jerry Cole was a confirmed alcoholic when he was sixteen years old. He always did whatever his feelings told him to do. Though he grew up in a Christian home where the high standards of God were practiced and taught, he became very rebellious at an early age and yielded himself to various sins. He reached a level of debauchery that took him into the gutter and to prison by the time he was eighteen. Unbelievably sordid stories came back to his parents and his pastor during those grim days of his life.

One day, in total desperation he cried out to God for deliverance and salvation. God miraculously worked in his life to grant the request of his heart. Now, four years later, Jerry speaks very clearly about the necessity of adhering to righteous regulations imposed by God. Since he has been forgiven, the righteousness of God is the rule of his life, and that rule is the theme of his song to those who are around him.

Resolution #3: Concerning Praise

The third resolution to break forth from David's lips has to do with praising God. When a man falls into sin, his first tendency is to blame God for the problems that brought about the sin or led to the failure. But when he is forgiven and restored, he desires to praise God for His mercy and grace. Like evangelism and the preaching of righteousness, praise to God must come from a *pure* heart.

Praise may find expression in sacrifice or testimony or prayer. But it finds its most natural and fullest manifestation in happy, musical expression. When God fills the heart with praise, He puts a new song in the mouth. According to Psalm 40:3, this joy breaks forth like the fresh rains of spring. On the basis of His forgiveness, David prayed that God would open his lips so he could praise and extol God for Who He is, for what He has done and for how He deals with men.

David selected praise as the most acceptable sacrifice to offer to God because God did not at that time want the sacrifice of animals upon a burning altar. Rather, He wanted the sacrifice of a broken spirit from the king, expressed with words of thanksgiving and exaltation.

Resolution #4: Concerning Sacrifices in Jerusalem

One final resolution came to the mind of the psalmist. He felt it necessary to make some statement about his worship and the worship of the people in the capital city of his kingdom. David's sin inhibited him in his witness, in his preaching of righteousness and in his praise to God. It also slowed the building of the city. The walls were not completed, the temple was not built and adequate opportunities for worship were not being furnished to the people of that city.

Because his sin had affected the progress in the city, King David requested a special blessing upon the internal workings of the city and strength to complete the building of the walls. The king resolved that when the walls were completed and blessing came to the city, the people would worship God through the offering of sacrifices. If this could be accomplished, David's heart would rest because through repentance, renewal and resolution the great scars of his sin would be removed. His own life, as well as the lives of his people could again be used to bring glory to the God of Heaven and earth.

Never forget that when sin enters your life, it is essential for you to recognize it, repent, confess it to God, seek the restoration of fellowship that is available to you and make resolutions that will lead you into renewed service for the King of Kings.

> Lord, speak to me, that I may speak
> In living echoes of Thy tone;
> As Thou hast sought, so let me seek
> Thy erring children lost and lone.
>
> O use me, Lord, use even me,
> Just as Thou wilt and when, and where,
> Until Thy blessed face I see—
> Thy rest, Thy joy, Thy glory share.

What Is Your Answer?

1. What two things did David request in order to be able to carry on a ministry of teaching transgressors and converting sinners?

2. Do you think these two things are essential elements in the ministry of your own life? Can you support this from the New Testament?

3. How is guilt related to singing?

4. What sacrifices does God want more than a burnt offering?

5. As you study verse 15, do you believe God prompts a mouth to be opened so it can praise Him?

6. What response should the goodness of God toward His children prompt from them?

7. Describe the various types of sacrifices in verse 19.

CHAPTER 7

Envy: An Enemy from Within

BIBLE PORTION TO READ: Psalm 73

LITTLE CAROL was embarrassed by her faded dress and well-worn shoes. She felt conspicuous at school because she did not look as nice as the other children. She heard her mother and father continually thank God for giving them so many blessings, such as health and strength and clothes to wear. She heard them rejoice in His faithfulness, and she was impressed by Matthew 6:33 when her father read it at the dinner table: "But seek ye first the kingdom of God, and his righteousness; and all these things shall be added unto you."

Her childish mind was disturbed, however. How could her parents be so godly and righteous and yet not have enough money to buy beautiful clothes for her like the naughty neighbor children wore? Their parents took the Lord's name in vain and went to wild parties on Saturday nights. She envied the fun and the many nice things those children had.

She determined that when she was older, she

would not go to church or read the Bible. She concluded it was foolish to be a Christian because ungodly people had more money and more fun than Christians.

This kind of thinking has been common through generations and has resulted in the downfall of multitudes of believers.

Asaph was a chief musician of David. He spent a great deal of time developing and leading music at worship services in Jerusalem. He, too, watched the people around him and noticed that the wicked prospered. This seemed contrary to God's promise of blessing upon the righteous.

Asaph's mind was disturbed, and his heart was filled with envy. He understood that God was good to Israel and to those who had a clean heart. But the prosperity of arrogant, wicked people was difficult for him to comprehend. Like little Carol, he was walking a treacherous path toward the rejection of his faith.

The Condition of Asaph

Asaph was a good musician, a man of great musical ability, organizational skill and prestige. In spite of all he enjoyed as the chief musician of David's day, he was bothered by the successes and power of certain people around him. He envied those who were unrighteous and unbelieving for possessing things he did not have. "My feet were almost gone," he said. It was as though he was on a slippery place and right on the edge of falling (v. 2).

The Christian should never envy the wicked no matter how much they prosper in this world.

"Whom have I in heaven but thee? and there is none upon earth that I desire beside thee. My flesh and my heart faileth: but God is the strength of my heart, and my portion for ever" (Psalm 73:25, 26).

John was a teenage farm boy who loved to trap and hunt, as had his older brothers. He wanted to be an even better trapper than his older brothers, and his efforts to excel led him into some dangerous places.

To set traps near some dens on a hillside, he climbed along a narrow path on a steep hill high above a limestone bluff.

One warm winter day, John decided to take a shortcut across the slick, snow-covered hill above the cliff. As he approached an extremely steep part of the slope, he began to slide on the snow. He slid for nearly sixty feet toward the edge of the cliff. In desperation he sprawled on the ground, spreading his legs and arms in an effort to stop himself. His heart was in his throat as he approached certain death.

Finally, his foot came to rest on a small bush only a few feet from the drop-off. Not until the late evening hours as the snow began to freeze once again was he able to make his way off the hillside to safety.

In a different sense the psalmist realized that he was in a treacherous, slippery position for envying the successful, wicked people of his day (vv. 2, 3).

In verse 3 he called the wicked people "foolish." This word is often used in the book of Proverbs to describe a person who is like a rowdy boy who walks through the halls of his school with his chest sticking out, banging into everybody. He has an arrogant, haughty spirit, without concern for other people.

The Causes of Envy

In verses 3-12 Asaph described in great detail the people he envied. They were sleek, well-fed people who sat at banquets and were not intimidated by others about them. They were prosperous and proud, often persecuting others and even making sarcastic statements about God Himself. They did not seem to have the troubles that other men had, nor were they plagued by famine or war. Asaph observed, "There are no bands in their death." They seemed to have painless, unencumbered deaths.

Asaph noted how the rich seemed to circumvent the problems of life. Their horses were well fed and well trained. They rode in fancy chariots that never broke down. Footmen walked before and behind them to protect them. Their granaries were filled with grain for any emergency. They had money to spare and connections so they could buy the very best.

In verse 6 Asaph exclaimed that they "wore" pride around their necks like a pendant for everyone to notice. Besides that, they "wore" violence like a garment. Their heartlessness and violence were openly demonstrated. Unafraid of the law or the consequences of their behavior, they were able to sap the lifeblood from others without worry. In verse 7 he described them as having eyes that stood out with fatness. They had more than their hearts could desire.

The Neiman-Marcus Company has a Christmas catalog for people who wish to buy Christmas presents for someone who has everything. The extraordinary gifts range in price from fifty dol-

Daily Bible Readings

Sunday—Warning Against Envy—Proverbs
  14:30; 24:1, 2, 19, 20
Monday—Just Desserts—Job 21:7-18
Tuesday—Victim of Envy—1 Kings 21:1-10,
  14
Wednesday—Two Kinds of Wisdom—
  James 3:13-18
Thursday—It Pays to Trust God—Jeremiah
  17:5-11
Friday—Do Your Duty—Ecclesiastes 12:1-
  8, 13, 14
Saturday—Maintaining Perspective—
  Psalm 100

lars to fifty-thousand dollars. To receive one of these gifts is a mark of belonging to the affluent segment of our society. Asaph had observed similar things in his day.

He also observed that these people were corrupt. He probably meant that they were corrupt in their minds. Out of their corrupt minds he observed they carried on high conversations about their oppression of other people. They held little conferences at which they discussed with satisfaction their harsh and cruel treatment of less fortunate people.

Asaph saw that they set their mouths against Heaven itself, challenging the rights of God. He observed, "Their tongue walketh through the earth," probably indicating that they spent considerable time talking about all of the places they had traveled, as well as their influence from coast to coast.

These rich, proud people had many followers who flocked after them, hoping to gain something by an association with them. Instead, however, the wealthy drained them and persecuted them. Even while they were doing it, they made sarcastic remarks about God, insinuating that it is impossible for Him to know what was going on and that probably He knew nothing at all (v. 11).

As Asaph looked at these self-sufficient, strong, proud, violent talkers, he realized that though they were very ungodly, they were prosperous as the world measures prosperity. They were better off than he was. His observation brought him to the same devastating conclusion little Carol reached.

The Confusion Caused by Envy

The conclusion of the psalmist was that his pure, godly life was all in vain (v. 13). He was plagued, chastened and troubled throughout every day. His faith in Jehovah was not paying off. As things looked to him, the world was better off than he.

Like many a believer with these kinds of doubts, Asaph hid them in his heart and continued to live his life in misery. His conclusions were simply too painful to meditate upon.

It is fortunate that the psalm does not end here and that Asaph also narrated his restoration from this pit of depression in which he found himself.

The Cures of Envy

Four distinct things brought Asaph out of his envious despair. First, he went into the house of God to hear the Word of God (v. 17). He had part in the music portion of the worship under King David, so it was common for him to return to the sanctuary where he could hear the Word of God taught.

Many a man of God has looked at the world and longed after the things of the world. Those who allow themselves to be sidetracked from going to church or Sunday School find it very difficult to combat envy. It is only when they return to a place where they sit under the teaching of God's Word that they begin to see the other side of the picture and realize that their righteous life and commitment to the King of Kings are worthwhile.

The second thing Asaph did was to reconsider the wicked man's future (vv. 18-20). This occurred while he was in the sanctuary where he was confronted by the teachers of the law. He noted that though they appeared to be prosperous, the wicked were actually standing in slippery places. He came to realize they were the ones hanging over the edge of the cliff. God would cast them down to destruction just as He had destroyed the hosts of Pharaoh in the Red Sea and had swallowed up Korah in the ground when he rebelled against Moses. God would cast down the ungodly as He did King Saul at the hand of the Philistines or Absalom in the oak tree. He would punish them as He did the Assyrians after their armies had ravaged the land of Israel.

The psalmist came to understand that lives of the wicked are like a dream. Dreams are without meaning or significance in the broad daylight of reality. Though dreams may bring pleasure or despair while they are occurring, they have no lasting value.

This brought Asaph to the third step in his cure of envy. Verses 21 and 22 tell us that he repented. Recognizing his foolishness and ignorance for thinking such envious thoughts, he lifted his eyes toward the blessings of God.

A fresh look at the presence and provision of God was the fourth step in Asaph's victory over envy. In verses 23-26 he pictured his position as a child of God. The father tenderly held his right hand to guide him through the course of his life without error or flaw. Even through troublous times and disconcerting days he was assured that the will of God was being accomplished in his life. He also knew that upon his death he would go into the presence of God. His success in life was no longer measured by the accomplishments of the wicked, but by the presence and care of his Savior. He could say with Job:

> For I know that my redeemer liveth, and that he shall stand at the latter day upon the earth:
> And though after my skin worms destroy this body, yet in my flesh shall I see God:
> Whom I shall see for myself, and mine eyes shall behold, and not another; though my reins be consumed within me (Job 19:25-27).

Every believer today needs to remember the story of the rich man and Lazarus in Luke 16:19-31. The rich man appeared to be prosperous; Lazarus was a beggar. But in the day of their death, Lazarus was exonerated and blessed because of his faith in God while the rich man died and was ushered into eternal destruction. That story keeps the major issues of life in clear perspective. The Christian should never envy the wicked no matter how much they prosper in this world. They do not have the blessing of God upon their lives, nor will they experience the presence of God throughout eternity.

> Praise the Savior, ye who know Him!
> Who can tell how much we owe Him?
> Gladly let us render to Him
> All we are and have.

What Is Your Answer?

1. Why did Asaph nearly fall? Do you think it is always wrong to watch the wicked?

2. What personal characteristics of the prosperous wicked did Asaph observe (vv. 4-7)?

3. How do prosperous wicked men speak and act toward God and His people (vv. 8-12)?

4. What conclusion did Asaph reach when he compared himself with the wicked (v. 13)? Do you think this is often the conclusion Christians reach when troubles fill their lives?

5. Where did Asaph go so that his attitude was abruptly changed?

6. What three things were true of the psalmist because he envied the wicked (v. 22)?

7. What conclusions does he draw about the wicked and himself (vv. 27, 28)?

CHAPTER 8

The Brevity of Life

BIBLE PORTION TO READ: Psalm 90

HERBS, EXERCISE and rest have all been recommended as possible ways to lengthen the days of men. Some men, such as Ponce de Leon, have even sought for a Fountain of Youth.

In 1521 the Spanish explorer Ponce de Leon led an expedition to Florida where he intended to found a colony and find the Fountain of Youth. Ponce de Leon did not discover the Fountain, nor did he establish a colony. He did receive a severe wound in a battle with the Indians, however, and retreated to Cuba where he died.

Though he drank water from every spring he came upon while exploring Florida, he never found the legendary Fountain, and he passed from this life through the door of death like all men.

Psalm 90 deals with the brevity of human life. It contrasts man's temporal existence with God's eternal life and draws them together with clarity.

Man Needs God Because of Life's Brevity

Before Moses, the writer of Psalm 90, discussed the brevity of man's life and the eternality of God, he said, "LORD, thou hast been our dwelling place in all generations." As he thought back through the generations of his ancestors, it became apparent that they had had no permanent dwelling place.

Abraham left Ur and dwelt in tents all the days of his life. Joseph and the other sons of Jacob eventually moved to Egypt where they lived as foreigners and finally slaves. During Moses' lifetime they fled from Egypt into the Sinai peninsula where they lived in a rocky, barren desert without any cities or houses. The land was so arid that daily manna and water from the rock were necessary to keep the pilgrims alive. As he thought back through the history of Israel, Moses knew God was the only permanent dwelling the nation ever had had.

Moses was thrilled by the thought that God Himself was their dwelling place. In verse 2 he established that God is "from everlasting to everlasting." In his mind he was tracing God back into the eternal past and stretching forward into the eternal future. It was consoling to realize that the children of Israel were dwelling in a habitation that was everlasting.

In contrast to the everlasting nature of God, man returns to the dust from whence he was taken. When Adam was created, he did not have the seeds of death in him. According to Genesis 2:7 he was formed from the dust of the ground, but there was no indication that he would return to the ground again.

Rather than struggling to live beyond our allotted days, we should endeavor to utilize the days we have to their best advantage.

A Verse to Memorize

"So teach us to number our days, that we may apply our hearts unto wisdom" (Psalm 90:12).

God warned the perfect man that he should not eat of the tree of the knowledge of good and evil because if he did, he would surely die (Gen. 2:17). After Adam fell, God pronounced a curse upon the man and concluded with these words: "In the sweat of thy face shalt thou eat bread, till thou return unto the ground; for out of it wast thou taken: for dust thou art, and unto dust shalt thou return" (Gen. 3:19).

Several figures in Psalm 90 illustrate the eternality of God and the brevity of man. Moses showed the eternality of God by saying that a thousand years are like yesterday when it is past. A thousand years to God make only a brief memory that lacks either length or detail. Moses said further that a thousand years are as a watch in the night to God. (A watch is a brief, four-hour span of time through which a man sleeps without awareness of its beginning or ending or the passing of time.)

Moses chose to illustrate the brevity of man's life by saying that God carries men away as a flood carries debris before it (v. 5). Any attempt to withstand the floodtide of God's pattern of life and death is fruitless. Man is "as a sleep"; man's life begins and ends without any sense of duration. Man is like grass that grows up with zest and vigor. At the height of its growth, it is cut down and withers away. The Grim Reaper, death, mows man to the ground. He spares no one. The time is brief between the growing and the mowing.

Several men in the Bible expressed this well. David said, "As for man, his days are as grass: as a flower of the field, so he flourisheth. For the wind passeth over it, and it is gone; and the place thereof shall know it no more" (Ps. 103:15, 16). In another place he observed, "Behold, thou hast made my days as an handbreadth; and mine age is as nothing before thee . . ." (Ps. 39:5). And the psalmist said, "For my days are consumed like smoke, and my bones are burned as an hearth" (Ps. 102:3). James said, ". . . For what is your life? It is even a vapour, that appeareth for a little time, and then vanisheth away" (James 4:14). Job said, "My days are swifter than a weaver's shuttle, and are spent without hope" (Job 7:6).

An Explanation for Life's Brevity

Having established that man's life is brief and God's life is eternal, Moses proceeded to give a reason for the brevity of man's life. His immediate conclusion, beginning in verse 7, is that man dies because of the anger of God. When God in His purity looked upon Adam and Eve in their sin, He pronounced condemnation upon them.

In Genesis 6:5-7 we have the record of God's evaluation of man prior to the Flood. He saw that the wickedness of man was great and that his thoughts were always evil. God was grieved and declared that He would destroy man whom He had created.

Sin against God brings the wrath and punishment of God. It results in severe punishment, even death. Habakkuk the prophet stated it well: ". . . O LORD, thou hast ordained them for judgment; and, O mighty God, thou hast established them for correction. Thou art of purer eyes than to behold evil, and canst not look on iniquity . . ." (Hab. 1:12, 13).

Daily Bible Readings

Sunday—Cause of Death—Genesis 3:1-6
Monday—One Never Knows—Luke 12:16-21
Tuesday—Walk in the Light—Ephesians 5:8-17
Wednesday—Vanishing Vapor—James 4:13-17
Thursday—Open the Door—Colossians 4:2-6
Friday—Because of the Times—1 Thessalonians 5:1-9
Saturday—Be Ye Steadfast—1 Corinthians 15:51-58

In His displeasure, God has limited the average life of man to seventy years. For some who are strong, life expectancy may be stretched to eighty years or more. If that is the case, those last years are filled with labor and sorrow. In many lands, old people struggle to eat, and they move about with agonizing frailty. Even in the United States, where careful facilities are maintained for senior citizens, old people sit in the loneliness of nursing homes without friend or family, too weak to enjoy life but afraid to die.

Petitions Prompted by Life's Brevity

Moses concluded he should not worry about the brevity of life, give up in despair or live a purely hedonistic existence. Instead, he asked several requests of God so that he could better utilize the days of his life for the glory of God. Every Christian should follow in these footsteps. Rather than struggling to live beyond our allotted days, we should endeavor to utilize the days we have to their best advantage.

Moses' first request was, "So teach us to number our days, that we may apply our hearts unto wisdom" (v. 12). This is a major consideration for everyone who recognizes the shortness of his life. Every day is important.

Jesus Christ set a perfect example of the use of time. He moved through His entire life with measured tread, never in a hurry but always certain He was accomplishing the perfect will of the Father. He was serene but serious as He worked according to His Father's plan. He knew that His life's calendar had been arranged before the foundation of the world; and through close communion with His Father, He received instructions as to the most minute details of His daily experience. In John 9:4 He declared, "I must work the works of him that sent me, while it is day: the night cometh, when no man can work." If time was important to Jesus Christ, it should be extremely important to Christians.

Someone has likened a twenty-four-hour day to a bank that credits every man's account each morning with $86,400. No balance is carried over from day to day. Every night at midnight any amount remaining is cancelled, and the next moment a fresh $86,400 is deposited.

Such a time bank exists for every individual. Every morning we are credited with 86,400 seconds. Each night the record is burned. No overdrafts are allowed. If a man fails to use the day's deposit, his loss is irrevocable. We must always determine the priorities of our days and seek the will of God without fail so that our lives will be well spent.

Moses made several other requests because of the brevity of life. He asked for renewed, sweet fellowship with God in verse 13. In verses 14 and 15 he pleaded for the mercy of God so that he might be able to rejoice with great joy. In verse 16 he asked God to visibly manifest Himself through His mighty works. And in verse 17a he pleaded for the favor or blessing of the Lord in his life and the lives of the Children of Israel.

His last request has powerful implications for every redeemed person. He asked, "Establish thou the work of our hands upon us." Many of us have stood upon the beach, watching adults and children build castles in the sand. With care and skill they erect marvelous structures with towers, moats, bridges and courtyards. Often children will sit nearby after the work of art is completed to protect it from people who may destroy it. But as the day wears on, the unstoppable tide begins to return upon the beach once again. As it does, the castle is washed away by the waves. Most of the things we accomplish in life are very much like sand castles. They do not last.

Moses' final prayer was that God would somehow cause the works of their hands to have lasting significance in a world where most things decay with use and time. The apostle Paul admonished Timothy, "Fight the good fight of faith, lay hold on eternal life, whereunto thou art also called, and hast professed a good profession before many witnesses" (1 Tim. 6:12). In another letter the old apostle declared that he had fought his fight well and finished the course that God had laid out for him: "Henceforth there is laid up for me a crown of righteousness, which the Lord, the righteous judge, shall give me at that day: and not to me only, but unto all them also that love his appearing" (2 Tim. 4:8).

A man of God can do many things that will last for all eternity. Every soul won to Jesus Christ will be an eternal monument to a faithful witness. Every child who grows up to be a godly adult and every brother or sister affected by the teaching of God's Word will be established forever. According to 1 Timothy 6:19 even the wise use of money can result in blessings throughout eternity. All of us should pray along with Moses, "Establish thou the work of our hands upon us."

What Is Your Answer?

1. What attribute of God is emphasized strongly in verses 2 and 4?

2. In verses 5 and 6 the psalmist named three examples of what men are like in relation to God. Give the three examples and think about how they illustrate the weakness and brevity of man.

3. What is the reason for man's brief life (vv. 7-9)?

4. What may a man expect from life if he lives beyond seventy years? Does this seem to be the pattern in life today?

5. What do you believe verse 12 means when it speaks of numbering our days so we may apply our hearts to wisdom? Do you believe you are doing this?

6. In what verse does the psalmist ask God to change His mind about His servants and their sin? Do you think this is a proper prayer for today?

7. For what two things does the psalmist pray in verse 17?

CHAPTER 9

Covered by His Care

BIBLE PORTION TO READ: Psalm 91

MOSES WAS responsible for leading over two million people from their comfortable homes in Egypt, across the Red Sea and into the wilderness of Sinai. The gardens of Goshen, with their leeks, garlic, melons and onions, lay far behind. The windswept sands of the desert stretched on every side. Barrenness, inadequate food and human enemies dogged the steps of the nation.

As weeks stretched into months, problems developed among the people. They quarreled about their rights. Pride and possessiveness caused feuds. During times of serious emergencies, Moses himself served as the mediator. He was often overwhelmed by the responsibility of such time-consuming counseling.

God had promised Moses that He would personally lead him and the Children of Israel to the Promised Land. God's presence was visible in the cloud by day and the pillar of fire by night. From time to time Moses desired to seek advice from God Himself. To accomplish this, he set up a tent on the outside of the camp where he often went to speak with Jehovah (Exod. 33).

On a clear day Moses could easily detect the approach of God because the shadow of the cloud fell across the door of the tent. When Moses entered the tent, the cloud in which God abode descended to the door, and God talked with Moses. As a leader of God's people, Moses sought advice and gained insight as he sat under the shadow of the Almighty.

Those experiences in the desert prompted Moses to pen Psalm 91. He began the psalm by saying, "He that dwelleth in the secret place of the most High shall abide under the shadow of the Almighty" (v. 1). Moses could say that because he had experienced it. Whenever he went to the secret place of inquiry and communion, God came so that the shadow of the cloud covered him.

God's Presence with Believers

God no longer dwells in a cloud, but every believer has the opportunity to know the personal presence of God when he goes to the secret place of prayer. Jesus promised the coming of the Comforter in John 14:13-17. (The word *Comforter* is translated from a Greek word which means "to come alongside.") The Holy Spirit of God in the believer today is the Comforter. He is the One Who comes alongside to bless, empower and give information about life. Jesus said, "Howbeit when he, the Spirit of truth is come, he will guide you into all truth . . ." (John 16:13). Every believer has his own "secret place of the most High" because the Holy Spirit of God is available to minister to him.

In verse 2 of Psalm 91 Moses painted three pictures of what God meant to him as he dwelt under the shadow of the cloud. He called Him his Refuge, his Fortress and his God. He looked upon God as his Refuge because He protected Moses from the storms of the desert, the heat of the sun, the driven sand and the wild animals that roamed the wilderness regions. No natural enemy could overcome Moses because he lived under the shadow of the cloud.

Moses called God his Fortress because He was like a tower or mountain castle where Moses was well guarded against the bitter attacks of men. No sword or arrow could harm him. Even the rebellion of Korah was in God's hands when "the earth opened her mouth, and swallowed them up, and their houses, and all the men that appertained unto Korah, and all their goods" (Num. 16:32).

Moses called Jehovah his God because God was his Creator and Sustainer, the Master of life and death. He saw God in each of these ways because he had spent much time in the secret place and had experienced the protection of God when enemies and elements would have destroyed a man without God.

God's Provision for Believers

Every person who experiences the presence of God in the secret place of prayer may expect God to take care of him. Moses recalled the things that such a child of God may expect. (1) He will be snatched from imminent danger as a bird is caught away from the snare of the fowler (v. 3a). God has the power to overrule when evil is threatened against His children. (2) Jehovah will also deliver him from the pestilence that destroys (v. 3b). Moses knew that God had preserved the Children of Israel from the terrible pestilences and plagues of the wilderness.

(3) God's protection will cover the child of God like a mother bird shelters her little ones from the night, animals, the hawk and the storm (v. 4a). The faithful child of God should expect similar protection from God. (4) The integrity of God will also be a shield and buckler, furnishing protection from the enemy who would kill (v. 4b). God's truth is an incomparable attribute. He cannot lie. Jesus called Himself the Way, the Truth and the Life (John 14:6).

(5) God promises to take away the terror of the night and the fear of the arrow during the day (v. 5). These surprise enemies will not strike fear in the heart of the person under God's cloud. (6) The great pestilences and plagues such as those in Egypt pose no problem when God is near (v. 6). (7) The man who lives under the cloud may expect to be invulnerable (v. 7). Though tens of thousands should fall all around him, he cannot be touched unless God permits.

William O. Cushing caught the sense of this psalm:

> Under His wings I am safely abiding,
> Tho the night deepens and tempests are wild;
> Still I can trust Him—I know He will keep me,
> He has redeemed me and I am His child.

Under His wings, O what precious enjoyment!
There will I hide till life's trials are o'er;
Sheltered, protected, no evil can harm me,
Resting in Jesus I'm safe evermore.

Occasionally a child wanders from his mother in a supermarket or department store. The first response of the little one is to quickly look for the missing parent. He runs up one aisle and down another as he begins to breathe faster and his eyes fill with tears. Suddenly he stops and begins to cry loudly. Fear and lostness fill his little mind. He has visions of never being restored to his mother's protection again. When the child of God wanders away from the secret place, he, too, experiences apprehension and a sense of lostness because he does not have close contact with the Heavenly Father.

God's Care for Believers

As Moses addressed the subject of God's care in verse 9, he restated the qualifications a man must possess in order to receive God's tender love. Once again he said a man must make God his refuge and his dwelling.

He continued with a list of the benefits of this closeness to God in verses 10-13. In verse 10 he said that no evil would befall this man, nor would any plague come near his dwelling. God *will* preserve from danger.

Moses stated that those who make God their refuge will be so well situated that the plague will not reach them (v. 10). They will be delivered from the presence as well as the power of the plague.

The protection of angels is promised in verses 11 and 12. Two angels journeyed to Sodom, and after having spent the night in Lot's house, they delivered him from the city before it was destroyed by the judgment of God. Even in our day, angels are ministering spirits who use their knowledge, strength, speed and time to preserve those who await the coming of the Lord Jesus Christ.

The care of God also furnishes strength for those who make God their refuge. This is a special strength that helps them overpower the lion, the adder and the dragon. For the dwellers in the desert, this was an important feature of God's concern for them.

A Divine Promise to Believers

The last three verses of this psalm record God's personal promises to each one who dwells in the secret place. His first promise is a promise of deliverance because such a child loves his Heavenly Father so much. Love draws; it does not repel. The love of a man for his God will draw him to the place of prayer.

We have all noticed how love draws a young woman toward her boyfriend. His response to her affection causes him to help her with her coat, assist her with her chair at the table and protect her when he takes her on a date. God is no less responsive to those who love Him. The simple words of the Lord Jesus Christ are "Come unto me, all ye that labour and are heavy laden, and I will give you rest" (Matt. 11:28). Paul proclaimed, "Whosoever shall call upon the name of the Lord shall be saved" (Rom. 10:13). These verses demonstrate that when a man sets his affection upon God, God responds with deliverance.

God's second promise is that He will honor and highly esteem the person who knows His name (v. 14b). *Jehovah* is the name of God. It reveals God as the ever-present One, eternal and available for those who need Him. The man who dwells under the cloud knows God well enough to understand the meaning of His name. Such intimacy causes God to elevate that individual to a place of respect and honor. The man who prays is assured of answers to his prayers, assistance in trouble, deliverance from problems, long life and the salvation of God.

Joe carried his well-filled lunch bucket every day of the school year. At noon he bartered his peanut butter and jelly sandwiches and traded his thermos of tomato soup for other kinds of food. He was tired of peanut butter sandwiches and tomato soup, but for some reason was bashful about telling his mother he did not like them. Every day for three years he traded or choked on what he could not trade.

How much better it would have been if he had simply approached his mother with his problem. She would have gladly packed something else in his lunch bucket. In the same way, many children of God fail to approach the Heavenly Father with their needs. As a consequence, they live in misery, distress and defeat.

Do you have a secret place of prayer? Does the Holy Spirit of God guide you into all truth? Do you experience the protection and care of God? If you cannot answer these questions with a hearty yes, why not find a quiet place where you can meet with God day after day in prayer, allowing Him to speak to your heart and furnish the gracious provisions He has waiting for you.

What Is Your Answer?

1. What one advantage is listed for abiding in the place of the most High?

2. What is significant about being under the shadow of the Almighty?

3. List some things from which the Almighty protects His own in verses 2-13.

4. List some of the names that the psalmist gives to God. What attributes do they describe?

5. How does the psalmist portray power in verse 13?

6. In verse 14 whom does God say He will deliver and set on high?

7. How will God satisfy the psalmist and show His salvation? Can I expect to be blessed like the psalmist?

CHAPTER 10

With God in the Midst

BIBLE PORTION TO READ: Psalm 114

The Fact of God's Presence

God is everywhere and knows everything. David
said there was no place he could visit in earth,
Heaven or hell to escape the presence of God (Ps.
139:7-9). God is present in the bustling city with
its millions of people, and in the loneliest island
of the world. God is omnipresent, present everywhere at all times.

With His omnipresence, God has the capacity
to be in certain places in a very special way. His
presence at the burning bush required Moses to
remove his shoes. On Mount Sinai it brought
thunder and lightning. His presence upon those
occasions had a much different effect than His
omnipresence had. In the same way, God is present with certain people or groups of people in a
unique way. Psalm 114 teaches that He took
Judah and Israel as a special dwelling place (v. 2).

The Holy Spirit also indwells individual believers, local churches and the universal Church.

The Christian is actually a sanctuary, a home of the Holy Spirit. The first occasion of such indwelling of the Holy Spirit occurred on the Day of Pentecost following the death and resurrection of Jesus Christ. Just prior to His death, the Lord had promised the Holy Spirit would come to do an unusual work in His disciples. He explained to them that the Spirit had dwelt with them but would shortly be living *in* them (John 14:17). Since that initial Pentecost, every believer has been a dwelling place of the Holy Spirit (1 Cor. 6:19, 20).

During times of distress or warfare, a child is often fearful of the dark. No sooner are the lights turned out than he begins to call for his mother or father. When the parent responds, "What do you want?" the child often replies, "I just wondered where you were." After a few minutes pass, the child may call to the parent, "Can you come and sit with me for a while?" The loving parent walks into the child's room and sits quietly on the side of the bed until the little one drifts off to sleep. The presence of the parent is all the child needs to feel secure and protected from the unseen enemies of his life.

God responded to Israel in very much the same way. He let them know He was abiding with them in the cloud by day and the fiery pillar by night. These were visible signs of an invisible God. Though He was omnipresent, Israel needed to *know* that He was specifically dwelling with

. . . God has given the earth and all of its blessings for the pleasure of mankind and for His own pleasure because He desires to dwell with us.

them. And in His grace, God gave them visible evidence of His presence.

Nature's Reaction to God's Presence

The Children of Israel had barely begun their trip toward the Promised Land when they arrived at the Red Sea. God assured Moses that He would divide the sea so the people could walk across on dry ground. A miracle took place. Because God was dwelling in the Children of Israel, supernatural power was available for their preservation.

Forty years later Joshua led them into the River Jordan during the rainy season when the river was overflowing its banks. God was present. He informed Joshua that the river would cease its flow and back up so that every member of the nation could cross on dry ground. The priests carried the ark of the covenant down to the river. As they stepped into the river, it stopped flowing. And as long as they stood in the middle of the river, no water passed by them. God's presence was available in each of these situations to control the water.

Peter, Andrew, James and John were fishermen. They had fished the Sea of Galilee all of their adult lives and understood that it was impossible to walk on water. One night during a vicious storm, the disciples rowed against the wind to no avail.

But the Son of God was present with them on the sea. When Jesus came walking to them on the water, Peter called to Him, "Lord, if it be thou, bid me come to thee on the water" (Matt. 14:28). Peter believed that if the Lord was there, he could actually get out of the boat and walk on the water. Though he took his eyes off Jesus and became afraid, the Lord reached out, caught him and took him safely to the boat.

As His death approached, Jesus told the disciples they would receive power after the Holy Ghost came upon them so they could be witnesses for Him throughout the entire world. With the coming of the Holy Spirit at Pentecost, that power became resident in the apostles. The power of the Holy Spirit of God Who lived in them took away their fear, doubts and failures and caused them to be outspoken witnesses of the resurrection, preachers of righteousness, builders of churches and writers of Holy Scripture.

Supernatural things occur in the lives of those who will gain their strength from the Holy Spirit. A Christian may actually experience victory over his own desires through the supernatural aid of the Spirit Who lives within him. In Galatians 5:16 the apostle Paul wrote, "This I say then, Walk in the Spirit, and ye shall not fulfil the lust of the flesh." God dwells with His children and works in their lives because He has a very special interest in them. They have been chosen from before the foundation of the world (Eph. 1:4).

Over fifty years ago a little boy discovered a secret retreat on a high hill among some giant trees near his home. Day after day he dreamed he was a strong woodsman who cut some of the big trees and built a cabin where he lived among the animals and birds with perfect contentment.

Whenever the lad had typical childhood difficulties, he walked to his special retreat to think and sometimes to cry. During his teen years he built a stone fireplace and cleared brush from among the trees. He walked to that spot one night after a revival service to bow his head and receive Jesus Christ as his personal Savior. At that same spot he sat to memorize Psalms 1, 23 and 100 and many other passages of Scripture.

As years went by, that man took special care of the quiet place on the hill. He built a picnic table and chairs and finally in his old age, a beautiful little cottage where he and his wife are spending happy years of retirement. Herman Webster fell in love with a special spot on the earth and has protected and improved it with his own hands.

In a similar way, God chose Israel. He dwelt among her, preserved her, improved her and directed her because she was pleasing to Him. He has also chosen the Church and dwells in it, showering it with blessings and productivity.

Questions Prompted by God's Presence

In verses 5 and 6 of this psalm, questions are addressed to the sea, the river, the mountains and the little hills. Why did they do unusual things for Israel? Why did they act in an unnatural way?

No answer is given in the passage, but the answer is clearly implied. They acted in supernatural ways because God commanded them to. God established the laws of nature, but He sometimes overruled them for the benefit of those with whom He dwelt. The pages of Scripture are filled with stories of the miraculous working of God in nature on behalf of those who loved Him. The mouths of lions were stopped for Daniel. Fire did not burn Shadrach, Meshach or Abed-nego. Ravens flew to feed Elijah; the heavens withheld their rain. The walls of Jericho fell to the ground. The sun stood still. Storms were calmed for the apostles. The blind were made to see. The lame were made to walk. And Jesus was born of a virgin. God often steps into the course of nature and alters events for the benefit of His own.

Because the Holy Spirit dwells in people, vast spiritual ministries have been accomplished. Revivals have brought entire cities to repentance. Saloons have been closed. Hundreds have accepted Jesus Christ by faith. Churches have been built all over the world because God has responded supernaturally on behalf of His own. Miracles take place because God is with us.

Recently I visited a home where a crippled grandmother sat, speaking with two of her teenage grandchildren. She was reminding them of the truths of this psalm as she sang softly:

> Be not dismayed whate'er betide,
> God will take care of you;

Beneath His wings of love abide,
God will take care of you.

It is God's interest in His children that causes Him to make nature bow in their best interests.

A Command Regarding God's Presence

Sometimes God completely changes the topography or function of the earth's surface. The last two verses of Psalm 114 present an illustration of this. God brought water out of the rock in the desert so that a river flowed through the camp of Israel, providing water for man and beast alike. Upon another occasion, molten lava and brimstone destroyed the cities of Sodom and Gomorrah.

Verse 7 expresses the command, "Tremble, thou earth, at the presence of the LORD, at the presence of the God of Jacob." The earth will always be an instrument God uses for the blessing or punishment of His created beings. He made a garden in Eden and filled it with all kinds of plants, trees and animals for the blessing of men. He told Adam to have dominion and to subdue every living creature. From that day until this, God has used the earth as a means of sustenance and blessing as well as punishment and regulation upon man.

The earth might well tremble at the presence of the God Who has absolute control over it. During the period of Great Tribulation, catastrophic events will happen in the earth. Earthquakes will be so widespread and devastating that every mountain and island will be moved from its place (Rev. 16:18, 20). One-third of the trees and all of the green grass will be burned (Rev. 8:7). One-third of the sea will be so polluted that all of its creatures will die (Rev. 8:8, 9).

During the very last days, every living thing in the ocean will die (Rev. 16:3). Great hailstones will fall out of heaven and destroy men (Rev. 16:21). The face of the earth's surface will be virtually flattened (Rev. 16:20). The earth will be almost totally obliterated because of God's punishment upon men.

Following the period of Great Tribulation, the millennial reign of Christ will transform the earth once again into a refreshing garden where the desert will blossom as the rose, waters will run pure and all of nature will be a blessing to man. Meat-eating animals will eat grass, and roses will be without thorns as the Son of God transforms chaos into order and failure into fruitfulness for the blessing of men once again.

After the millennial reign of Christ, the heavens and earth will be completely destroyed by fire. Peter describes the events of that day when he says, "But the day of the Lord will come as a thief in the night; in the which the heavens shall pass away with a great noise, and the elements shall melt with fervent heat, the earth also and the works that are therein shall be burned up" (2 Pet. 3:10).

Revelation 21:1—22:7 describes a new heaven and earth. It will be made by God as a dwelling place for righteous men throughout the ages of eternity where God will dwell in the midst of His own in harmony and purity. God created the world for our benefit, and He will create the new world for our benefit also. It is little wonder the psalmist said, "Tremble, thou earth."

A wealthy lumberman gathered rare woods from all over the world and had them delivered to a small village in upstate New York. He brought limestone, slate and tile from hundreds of miles. Then he hired expert builders to erect a mansion with large rooms, open stairways, servants' quarters, ballroom, cedar closets, rare tables and hand-crafted furniture.

One day he took his wife and two small children to the beautiful home. The young mother was overwhelmed at the beauty of the house. Every detail was exquisite, and every convenience was available. After they had toured the home, the lumberman turned to his wife and said, "Honey, it is for you." She nearly lost her breath with amazement and asked, "Why did you build such a beautiful home?" His reply was simple yet profound, "I love you, and I want to live here with you so I built it for our pleasure."

In the same way, God has given the earth and all of its blessings for the pleasure of mankind and for His own pleasure because He desires to dwell with us.

What Is Your Answer?

1. Where did God dwell as Israel journeyed from Egypt?

2. How did nature respond to God's presence with the Children of Israel?

3. Who turned the flint into fountains of waters?

4. Do you think God simply uses natural forces to accomplish His will, or is there a miraculous element in it? Explain your answer.

5. According to Genesis 1 and 2, do you believe God intended all of nature to be used for the benefit of mankind?

6. List several instances in which God controlled nature to protect, discipline or assist His children in a clearly supernatural way.

7. Do you think we can ever expect God to interact with nature to produce a miracle that will benefit a child of God in our generation?

CHAPTER 11

Working with God

BIBLE PORTION TO READ: Psalm 127

EVERY CHILD at some time or another has pulled away from his parents, saying, "I want to do it by myself!" Many times those are dangerous words; the independence-minded youngster falls down the stairs, tips over in his chair or spills his soup because he needs the superintending assistance of his mother.

Some folks never seem to get over the idea of wanting to do everything by themselves. As they grow into adulthood, they do not want the advice of experts nor the assistance of God in planning and carrying out their lives.

In Psalm 127 David composed some clear advice for his son. The main thrust of this brief musical admonition is that to pursue the activities of life without allowing God to work through them is meaningless and empty. Three times David calls it vanity.

Building with God

David wanted to build a building for God, but Jehovah had told him he had shed too much blood in great wars and therefore could not build a house to the name of God. God promised David that a son would be born to him who would be a man of peace and that his son would build the temple. David relayed this message to Solomon many years later with a word of exhortation:

> Now, my son, the LORD be with thee; and prosper thou, and build the house of the LORD thy God, as he hath said of thee.
> Only the LORD give thee wisdom and understanding, and give thee charge concerning Israel, that thou mayest keep the law of the LORD thy God (1 Chron. 22:11, 12).

David could have built the house of God if he had chosen to do so. He had the manpower, knowledge and material. But it would have been a vain building. The glory of God would never have come to fill it, and the dedication would have been an empty ceremony. When Solomon completed the building of the temple, however, it was a much blessed building because God was in it.

Jack London was a celebrated writer, well-known for books such as *The Call of the Wild* and short stories like "To Build a Fire." The early days of his life were filled with turmoil and insecurity. He was taunted by his friends for being illegitimate; his mother often moved from place to place; and while he was still a teenager the full responsibility for his family came to rest upon his shoulders.

Even in adulthood, Jack London was plagued

Without God, the greatest security is useless. With God, meager security is enough.

---

by troubles. He traveled on land and sea, looking for fulfillment and satisfaction. Finally, he began to build a lovely home. Vast amounts of his labor, money and time were spent erecting a building he imagined would bring satisfaction into his life. At last it was completed. Before one night had passed, however, fire burned it to the ground. Nothing remained of the building he hoped would be gratifying to his troubled heart. Jack London was not a Christian. He approached life as a humanist, without faith in Jesus Christ, seeking no advice from God or His Word. Great was his vanity because he built without God.

Defending with God

City streets are filled with policemen; night watchmen walk their regular patrols through vacant factories; the coast guard patrols thousands of miles of our shoreline; burglar alarms and watchdogs protect many affluent homes; and soldiers stand on guard duty throughout the world. Yet David said, "Except the LORD keep the city, the watchman waketh but in vain" (v. 1b). Safety and protection come from the Lord. His presence guarantees the well-being of His children, and no amount of human protection can guarantee security if God is not in it.

An ancient Greek legend tells how the small states of Greece united in a war to destroy Troy. The war continued for ten years outside the walls of the city until the Greek hero Ulysses thought of a way to enter the city. The Greeks built a huge wooden horse and told the Trojans that it was a gift for the goddess Athena. Then the Greeks sailed away.

The Trojans eventually opened their gates to look at the wooden horse. Finally they brought it into the city with joy and celebration. During the night of revelry, Greek soldiers hidden inside the horse opened the gates of Troy, and the Greeks returned to kill the Trojans and burn the city. All of their military might and city walls did not save the Trojans.

A Biblical illustration of the vanity of defenses established without God is found in the fall of the great city Babylon. Nebuchadnezzar had built what he considered to be an impregnable fortress. The walls were over 300 feet high and surrounded enough land to make the city self-contained. A huge moat surrounded the walls, and a river flowed through the middle of the city to furnish water for everyone. A bridge only 30 feet wide crossed the moat to the city where defense towers awaited any enemy who approached.

During the night of revelry Belshazzar, Nebuchadnezzar's son, saw handwriting on the wall that informed him of the destruction of the city (Dan. 5). That very night, Darius, king of the Medes, diverted the river so his soldiers could march beneath the city walls unhindered. Belshazzar and all his family and guards were killed in spite of the military defenses set up to protect him. Without God on his side, nothing could save him. Without God, the greatest security is useless. With God, meager security is enough.

Laboring with God

David warned Solomon that it was also vain to

Daily Bible Readings

Sunday—Building without God—Genesis
11:1-9

Monday—The Sleep of Peace—Psalm 4:6-8

Tuesday—Joint Effort—Acts 9:10-16

Wednesday—Warning and Promise—
Proverbs 22:6, 15; 29:15

Thursday—Our Part in Answered Prayer—
1 Peter 3:1-7

Friday—Filial Responsibility—1 Timothy
5:4, 16

Saturday—Parents and Children—
Ephesians 6:1-4

rise up early and labor all day without God (v. 2).
He was not recommending laziness or slothful-
ness; he was teaching that no amount of hard work
will produce contentment unless God is in it.

The last phrase of verse 2 says, "So he giveth his
beloved sleep." This phrase is difficult to understand but probably means that God takes care of
His beloved even when they are asleep.

Do you know what God does for you when you
are asleep? Your lawn keeps growing; your garden
keeps growing; your body rests; your children
grow; and your money earns interest. God keeps
giving even when you are at rest. How very important it is to make the God Who performs marvelous things both while you are awake and asleep
the center of your life and labors. To do otherwise
is the height of vanity.

The first chapter of Haggai records an illustration of vain labor. In verse 6 Haggai reminded the
people that they had sown much but harvested
very little. They had eaten but were not filled.
They had earned wages but had put them in bags

with holes. Their labors were fruitless.

> Go up to the mountain, and bring wood, and
> build the house; and I will take pleasure in it, and
> I will be glorified, saith the LORD.
> You looked for much, and, lo, it came to
> little; and when ye brought it home, I did
> blow upon it. Why? saith the LORD of hosts.
> Because of mine house that is waste, and ye
> run every man unto his own house.
> Therefore the heaven over you is stayed
> from dew, and the earth is stayed from her
> fruit (Hag. 1:8-10).

It is important to work with God in accomplishing the will of God. Labor that is selfishly contrived and selfishly oriented is vain.

Raising a Family with God

In the first two verses of Psalm 127, David took a negative approach. He spoke of things that were in vain. In the last three verses, however, he took a positive approach toward the subject of the family. His emphasis was upon children.

Children are a present from God. Children are a heritage and a reward from God (v. 3). They come into this world because God permits them to be born. They are a special inheritance from Him. Today people rebel against unwanted pregnancies. They talk about children being a drag on their lives. Abortion is an everyday occurrence, and selfish attitudes of the adults in a family hinder the development of the children and even lead to physical abuse.

A family sat around the Christmas tree, opening a vast array of presents. One at a time each gift was unwrapped by its recipient and displayed to the family. As little Susie opened the box that contained a special present from her mother, the mother's eyes sparkled with expectation. Susie reached in the box and pulled a doll from its wrapper. She held it high so she could see it. But a frown came across her face. "This isn't the one I wanted," she said with apparent disgust. The sparkle in her mother's eyes was replaced by hurt and rejection as she realized that her thoughtful efforts had not pleased her child.

God gives special gifts to moms and dads all over the world. They are tiny infants wrapped in a human mother and delivered to the family from God. Don't forget, God has given you your children. They are as He wanted them to be. Don't furrow your brow and say, "This is not the kind I wanted." Thank God for every one of them because they are His gift to you. They are a heritage of the Lord. Children are not some kind of regrettable blessing. They are not a penalty; they are a present. They are not a regret; they are a reward. Those who think otherwise are doubtful of the blessing and purpose of God.

Children are extensions of a family. In ancient days archers were an important part of the army. By using arrows, they were able to attack men some distance away. Every archer carried a quiver filled with arrows. The more arrows he had in his possession, the greater his ability to engage in combat at a distance. So vital was the possession of arrows that a soldier would often gather up arrows from the battlefield in order to keep his quiver filled.

In verse 4 David told his son that children in the home of a young father are like arrows in the hand of a mighty man. As they grow, they give the man an extension into the community. They are working units that help the home and protect the interests of the family. More than that, they give the parent the ability to project himself into the next generation. As the parent grows older and finally dies, the child, like an arrow, will fly on through time, leaving his mark and bringing glory to God in the place of his parent.

Nearly a century ago Christian Burke wrote the words of a hymn that speak the truth of this idea.

> Lord of life and King of glory,
> Who didst deign a child to be,
> Cradled on a mother's bosom,
> Throned upon a mother's knee:
> For the children Thou hast given
> We must answer unto Thee.
> May we keep our holy calling
> Stainless in its fair renown,
> That, when all the work is over
> And we lay the burden down,
> Then the children Thou hast given
> Still may be our joy and crown.

The parent who realizes God has given him an opportunity to project himself throughout his community and also into a future generation will be challenged to take special care in rearing his children because they represent him wherever they go.

Children are sources of happiness. In 1963 Frank Gilbreth and Ernistine Carey published a book entitled *Cheaper by the Dozen*. It was the story of their parents who had a dozen children, six boys and six girls. The account of their growing-up years is filled with laughter, enthusiasm and accomplishment. Their father certainly had a quiver full of arrows. His children made him happy as they extended his family throughout the community. He trained them with deliberate care so they would be good extensions of himself into the next generation.

A family brings happiness and accomplishment that no other success can produce. Money, buildings and great businesses cannot accomplish what children can when the parents rear them in the nurture and admonition of the Lord and plant in their hearts a desire to accomplish great things for God.

Children are protection for parents. Psalm 127 ends by stating that children "shall speak with the enemies in the gate." God told Abraham that his seed would possess the gates of their enemies. That meant that they would be victorious in warfare and would sit in the gates of the city, passing judgment upon the affairs of the people.

If children are properly trained, prepared and equipped to be successful, victorious accomplishers of great things for God, they will one day sit in places of responsibility as representatives of their parents.

A young pastor recently spent several hours counseling two parents. Both the father and mother were successful in the business world, having built a corporation that reached across the United States. In spite of such success, parental mistakes had produced rebellion and insensitivity to authority in their children. The teenagers had become involved in deep sin that threatened to destroy their own lives and the reputation of the family.

As the broken mother and father left his office, the pastor took his pen and wrote across a card lying on his desk, "No success in life can compensate for failure in the home." That is exactly what David was teaching his son Solomon in Psalm 127. Vain pursuits will never replace the warmth and happiness of a family living in the will of God.

What Is Your Answer?

1. In verses 1 and 2 what three activities of life are said to be vain if God is not working with the person who does them?

2. In verse 3 what are children called?

3. How do you think arrows and children are alike?

4. Does verse 5 indicate that several children may produce happiness?

5. Is a home with Christian parents a guarantee that children will be godly?

6. Is the old saying, "Early to bed and early to rise makes a man healthy, wealthy and wise" a good statement in the light of this psalm?

7. For whom was this psalm written?

CHAPTER 12

Wholehearted Praise

BIBLE PORTION TO READ: Psalm 138

THE LAST package of psalms written by David begins with Psalm 138. There are eight psalms in this series, running from 138 through 145. Some people do not understand that many of the psalms were written long after David had died. Psalm 137, for instance, talks about the captives sitting by the rivers of Babylon during the 70 years of captivity under Nebuchadnezzar. That means it was written at least 450 years after David's time.

This does not deny verbal inspiration, nor does it destroy the authenticity of the book of Psalms. It does help the reader understand that not every psalm was written by David. God gathered the psalms from a variety of writers and ages into a single book of Hebrew verse for instruction, edification and blessing for believers of all ages.

Psalm 138 is a psalm of praise. David had been a shepherd boy whose older brothers went to war as soldiers of Saul. God blessed him with special physical prowess during his training as a shepherd. With his bare hands he killed a lion and a bear. At the same time, David possessed a sensitive spirit and musical ability. During long hours of watching the flocks, he wrote music, played the harp, practiced with his sling and worshiped God.

He made his debut as a military man by felling Goliath with a rock and beheading the giant with his own sword. He accomplished all of this as a shepherd lad while his older brothers watched. From that day forward, David rose to a position of prestige, military power and spiritual sensitivity throughout the reign of King Saul.

King Saul became jealous of David's reputation and popularity and finally endeavored to take David's life. He pursued David through the hills, driving him into exile. David waited with patience and reliance upon God until one day the prophet Nathan walked into his presence with a message from Jehovah.

After briefly rehearsing David's past, the prophet of God told David his name would become like the names of the greatest men of the earth and that Israel would be settled in a home of their own, no longer to be disturbed. Wicked men would oppress them no more; and the land would be at rest. Nathan also gave David some special personal promises. The first was that God would build a house for David, not a physical house but a family. Nathan also told David that his family would continue to sit upon the throne of Israel and would have dominion over the kingdom forever.

David responded with great praise to God, calling Him the sovereign Lord and the Lord Almighty, God of Israel. He thanked God for His promises and committed himself to the full service of Jehovah during all of his life. It was at that time that the words of this psalm came to David's mind. This song records his reaction to God's special blessing upon him.

A Verse to Memorize

"I will praise thee with my whole heart:
before the gods will I sing praise unto thee"
(Psalm 138:1).

The Extent of David's Praise

It was customary for David to praise the Lord.
In Psalm 34:1 he said, "I will bless the LORD at all
times: his praise shall continually be in my
mouth." Every believer has a responsibility to
praise God in every circumstance.

A preacher in the early years of the United States
was kicked in the jaw by his horse. Unable to eat
solid foods, and suffering from excruciating pain,
the preacher was heard to say, "Praise God! That
horse could have kicked my head off."

Believers should learn to praise God during
trials because these trials bring patience and per-
fection into their lives. A far more serious tendency among believers is their neglect of praise to
God even when He *blesses* them. Somehow, they
assume credit for the good things and blame God
for the bad. David was not such a man. His heart
was committed to praise God for the good things,
and he did that throughout Psalm 138.

David's praise to God is characterized by intensity, boldness, the proper direction and the proper
Object. David was not halfhearted about his
praise. It involved his whole being. The intensity
of his praise is reflected in the opening words of
Psalm 138:1: "I will praise thee with my whole
heart. . . ."

An old story is told about a young man who fell
in love with a young lady who lived on an adjoin-
ing farm. He wrote a letter to her, expressing the

strength of his love. "I would swim the widest ocean for you," he said. "I would climb the highest mountain or cross the widest desert to share my love with you." Page after page followed in which he extolled the depth of his commitment. Finally, he signed his name. A brief PS followed: "I would like to ride over to your house for a visit next Saturday evening if it does not rain." The half-heartedness of his commitment was apparent. Needless to say, the young woman was not impressed.

In a similar way, the Christian must be careful he does not get caught up with praises that come from an insincere heart. David praised God with all of his heart, and we should do the same.

David was determined to praise God boldly. He said, "Before the gods will I sing praise unto thee" (v. 1b). In David's day the land of Palestine was filled with idols made by the hands of men and worshiped as gods. So thankful was David for what Jehovah had promised him that he would not hesitate to declare his praises in any religious setting. Like the apostle Paul, who was never ashamed of the gospel of Christ, the great king of Israel boldly declared his confidence in Jehovah.

The strength of David's praise is clearly demonstrated by his willingness to declare it regardless of what other people would think. Many times we are willing to praise God in the quietness of our own closet or in church, but we say very little in praise to God on the streets. The measure of the maturity of our praise rests with our ability to declare it openly before those people who may not be godly.

David directed his praise toward the holy place of God. His custom was to bow for worship toward the place of God's dwelling. Just as the Children of Israel bowed toward the tabernacle before David's day, and Daniel bowed toward Jerusalem while he was a captive in Babylon, so David humbled himself before the Lord by bowing toward the holy place. He put himself in the proper position before the Lord; he never exalted himself or other men under the guise of praising God. He was certain that those who observed him understood that he was praising God and God alone.

The fourth way David revealed the extent of his praise was that he praised God by His proper name, Jehovah. He did not use shallow, cheap, meaningless phrases to describe the God of Heaven and earth.

The name of God is extremely important to believers today as well. Often people will talk about Jesus. They use that simple name rather than referring to Him as the Lord Jesus Christ. The Second Person of the Trinity is more than Jesus. He is Jesus the Christ, and He is the Lord Jesus

Christ. Whenever someone praises the Second Person of the Trinity, he should say more than "I love Jesus," or "Jesus did this for me," or "Jesus did that." One who offers praise should also understand His eternal relationship with Israel and see how the Lord Jesus Christ fulfills God's plan as Savior, King and coming Judge.

The Content of David's Praise

The major portion of Psalm 138 contains a list of the things David was thankful for. While this list does not serve as a comprehensive model for praise to God, it does indicate those things that came to David's mind as he reflected on God's faithfulness and His promises for the future.

God's personal characteristics. As David contemplated what God had done for him, two attributes of God stood out above all the rest. They were loving-kindness and truth (v. 2). In His loving-kindness, God chose to use David as His royal representative to the nation Israel. David was grateful for this special calling. He was also thankful for God's truth because it reassured him that the things God told him in His loving-kindness would come to pass.

God does not make promises He will not keep, nor does He act kindly but with ulterior motives. His truth will not permit Him to be inconsistent or deceptive.

Answered prayer. David said, "In the day when I cried thou answeredst me" (v. 3a). A little chorus says:

> God hears and He answers pray'r;
> Cast on Jesus your every care,
> ....

> Hasten to take Him your problems,
> For God answers prayer.

Immediately after Nathan had given David God's promises about the establishment of his kingdom, the king prayed a serious prayer that concluded with these words:

> And now, O Lord GOD, thou art that God, and thy words be true, and thou hast promised this goodness unto thy servant:
> Therefore now let it please thee to bless the house of thy servant, that it may continue for ever before thee: for thou, O Lord GOD, hast spoken it: and with thy blessing let the house of thy servant be blessed for ever (2 Sam. 7:28, 29).

God's promised blessing began immediately. As days went by, the borders of David's kingdom were enlarged, his enemies were subdued and his family grew. God answered his prayer.

Giving strength. The strength that David received was not strength of military might but strength in his soul. Warfare, betrayal and death threatened the king constantly. But outside circumstances did not destroy his inner strength. He praised God continuously for strengthening him in his inner man.

Often young people have a weak or broken spirit that renders them unable to cope with life's situations in spite of their strong bodies. Without strength in their souls they accomplish little and possess no zest for life.

On the other hand, great saints of God who are old and dying possess a vigorous determination that carries them through their remaining days and into the portals of Heaven with joy and rejoicing.

Future world dominion among men. David began this word of praise by saying, "All the kings of the earth shall praise thee, O LORD . . ." (vv. 4, 5). This praise has unusual prophetic implications. One day David's Greater Son will be the King of all the earth. In that day, all the Gentiles will praise Him as He controls everything from economics to ecology.

God's attitude toward men. David rejoiced that God knew the hearts of men and that He honored the lowly and condemned the proud (v. 6). The apostle Peter echoed with the words, "God resisteth the proud, and giveth grace to the humble" (1 Pet. 5:5c). Even as God assisted Saul in his humility, He rejected him in his pride. Christ justified the humble publican rather than the proud Pharisee when both went to the temple to pray.

God's attitude toward pride has not changed. He still despises it even when it manifests itself in church members or pastors. He also has respect for the humble and will exalt them at an appropriate time. Every Christian should thank God and praise Him for His reaction to the humble and the proud.

God's constant preservation. David walked in the midst of constant trouble, but he experienced the protection of God (v. 7). That protection came to him in two distinct ways. Often he experienced the supernatural working of God so that he was able to accomplish acts of might beyond his normal ability. At other times God thwarted his enemies so they were unable to accomplish what they ordinarily could have done. Whether it was working out His will in David himself or thwarting the efforts of the enemy, God was preserving His own.

God's eternal faithfulness. David's final word of praise expressed his complete confidence that God would finish the work which He had begun (v. 8). The lives of some people are characterized by many starts but few finishes. This characteristic is so prevalent that corporations spend millions of dollars looking for executives who possess enough strength of character and determination to complete projects.

God finishes what He starts. Romans 11:29 says, "For the gifts and calling of God are without repentance." Hebrews 12:2 says, "Looking unto Jesus the author and finisher of our faith. . . ." Philippians 1:6 confirms this characteristic of God when it says, "Being confident of this very thing, that he which hath begun a good work in you will perform it until the day of Jesus Christ."

God is not a quitter in any of His projects. He made promises to Abraham that will be fulfilled. He planned redemption from before the foundation of the world and will see it through. He has set a course for your life, and He will furnish grace, strength and determination so that you can arrive at His desired goal. Praise Him for it!

What Is Your Answer?

1. How did David say he would praise God and where?

2. What reasons does the psalmist give for praising God's name in verses 2 and 3?

3. How can we be certain that God's Word is powerful and convincing?

4. What are two reasons in verses 4 and 5 that the kings of the earth will sing praises to God?

5. For whom does the Lord show the most respect? How can you be sure you are respected by God?

6. List some ways that God would take care of the psalmist when he was walking in trouble.

7. Give one reason why the psalmist was confident God would not forsake him.

CHAPTER 13

Singing a Happy Song

BIBLE PORTION TO READ: Psalm 147

PRAISE SONGS have been a part of the music of
the church from its earliest days. The "Doxol-
ogy," so familiar in many of our services, has been
sung since the late seventeenth century. Its words
of praise have become a pattern for Christians who
wish to exalt God for all He is and all He does.

> Praise God, from whom all blessings flow;
> Praise Him, all creatures here below;
> Praise Him above, ye heavenly host;
> Praise Father, Son, and Holy Ghost.

When a person feels like praising God, he usually feels like singing. Praise and song go together.
Since God should be exalted frequently by Christians through the medium of praise, songs of
praise should make up a large segment of Christian music.

Every believer should take time to evaluate what
he sings in order to make sure his songs are not
self-centered or praising man instead of God. The

writer of Psalm 147 exhorted or commanded his readers to praise God in song. The first command is given in verse 1, the second command in verse 7, and the third command in verse 12. After each exhortation the psalmist described the activities of God that should elicit praise from His children.

In each of these divisions he also presented a contrast. In verse 6 he said, "The LORD lifteth up the meek: he casteth the wicked down to the ground." This contrast shows the way God deals with the attitudes of different people. In verses 10 and 11 he said, "He delighteth not in the strength of the horse: he taketh not pleasure in the legs of a man. The LORD taketh pleasure in them that fear him, in those that hope in his mercy." These verses show that God is not influenced by a display of strength, but rather by respect.

In verses 19 and 20 the psalmist gave another contrast: "He sheweth his word unto Jacob, his statutes and his judgments unto Israel. He hath not dealt so with any nation: and as for his judgments, they have not known them. Praise ye the LORD." In this passage he contrasted God's revelation to Israel with the lack of revelation to the other nations.

As we analyze this psalm we will look at each command and then the reasons for singing.

The First Command to Sing

The psalmist defended his command to sing with three concise statements. He said, "It is

---

Though life's problems surpass the understanding of God's people and surprises startle them, God is never confused or amazed. He is to be praised for His infinite knowledge.

---

good," "It is pleasant," and "It is comely [beautiful]."

The Reasons for Singing

The psalmist explained that God cares for many things in a special way. He takes special interest in those who are meek or mourning because of the loss of material things.

God cares for the broken and dispersed. The psalmist declared that God deserved praise because He built up Jerusalem and regathered Israel's dispersed people (v. 2). Under Zerubbabel and Ezra the Jewish captives in Persia returned to rebuild the temple and later the walls of Jerusalem. Israel was once again dispersed after that restoration. God has patiently, carefully and protectively led the Children of Israel back to Palestine upon several occasions. After the Great Tribulation He will once again gather them from the four corners of the earth, and Jerusalem will be rebuilt. God cares about the dispersed and broken; He should be praised for this goodness.

God cares for the troubled. "He healeth the broken in heart, and bindeth up their wounds" (v. 3). God not only restores the physical needs of people and regathers them from their dispersion, but He can and does effectively work within them to bring about emotional and spiritual healing.

Believers today should praise God for His ability to heal the brokenhearted. They should sing songs such as "Be Still, My Soul" to remind themselves of God's ability to take care of the weary and grieved soul of a man.

God cares for the universe. The psalmist explained that God not only cares for the external and internal problems of men, but He also cares for the universe as a whole (v. 4). He actually knows the numbers of the stars and calls them by name. The psalmist properly exhorted his listeners to sing praises to God because of God's care and interest in wide expanses beyond us.

Christians today may respond to God's omnipotence with such great songs as "How Great Thou Art" and "I Sing the Mighty Power of God."

> I sing the mighty pow'r of God
> That made the mountains rise,
> That spread the flowing seas abroad
> And built the lofty skies.
> I sing the wisdom that ordained
> The sun to rule the day;
> The moon shines full at His command,
> And all the stars obey.

God cares with complete understanding. Jehovah's care is based upon full understanding of every situation (v. 5). Though life's problems surpass the understanding of God's people and surprises startle them, God is not confused or amazed. He is to be praised for His infinite knowledge.

Some songs of the church that will assist believers in praising God for His understanding are "God Is Love; His Mercy Brightens," "Join All

Daily Bible Readings

Sunday—Instruments of Music—Psalm 150
Monday—The Songs of the Spirit—
  Ephesians 5:18-20
Tuesday—A Song of Triumph—Judges
  5:1-12
Wednesday—The Song of Praise—Psalm
  40:1-3
Thursday—When Singing Is Gone—Amos
  8:1-8
Friday—The Memory of a Song—Psalm
  77:1-6
Saturday—Cause for Singing—1 Samuel
  2:1-10

the Glorious Names" and "Praise Ye the Lord, the Almighty." These songs extol God. Various parts of them praise Him for His wisdom and understanding, which exceeds the mind of mere mortals.

God cares for the meek and casts down the wicked. Songs should pour forth from the hearts of God's humble children because God is not put off by humility nor impressed by pride (v. 6). He is drawn to the lowly of heart and stands against the arrogant.

Christians should sing praises for God's care for the meek. Such songs as "The King of Love My Shepherd Is" and "God Will Take Care of You" praise God for His tender interests in His children. A great hymn like "A Mighty Fortress Is Our God" makes it clear that God also stands against the arrogant enemies of His children, destroying the foe and preserving the faithful.

The Second Command to Sing

In the command given in verse 7, the voices of men blend with the harp. Musical instruments played an important part in the music of Israel. In Psalm 150 the trumpet, timbrel, stringed instruments, organs, loud cymbals and psaltery are all mentioned as instruments to be used in the praise of Jehovah.

The word *sing* in verse 7 indicates an answer or response. This kind of singing reacts to the Lord for what He has done. His goodness to the Israelites called for appropriate praise in the form of music.

The Reasons for Singing

Along with the second command the writer offered another listing of blessings for which God should be praised. In this case he was thinking of ordinary operations of life on earth. He mentioned such things as rain, grass and the care of birds and animals. Such ordinary things of life are good topics for praise.

God provides rain. Verse 8 lists a sequence of events beginning with the formation of clouds and ending with the making of grass to grow in the mountains. In a clear, sunny sky the Lord forms clouds in order to bring the rain so grass will grow. Ordinarily, the believer looks upon this as being a process of nature. But in fact it is the superintending care of God.

Familiar songs for the Christian to sing in response to the psalmist's command to praise God for the rain are "I Sing the Mighty Power of God" and "All Creatures of Our God and King."

God provides food. Special emphasis is given to the "beasts" and to the "young ravens which cry" (v. 9). Though the animals that live upon the mountains store no food for winter, God takes care of them as well as the helpless little birds who appeal to their parents with loud crying. Once again the hymn "All Creatures of Our God and King" serves as a musical medium to exalt God for His provision to men and beasts alike.

God is not influenced by earthly power. Music that praises God should also be offered for God's attitude toward men and beasts. God is not influenced by the might of man or the strength of a horse. He has no dependence upon outside power because He is omnipotent. The earth and everything in it were made by Him, including the unmeasured energy of the sun and a million stars larger than the sun.

God's great pleasure is "in them that fear him" and place their confidence in His mercy. Regardless of his strength or accomplishments, when a man turns to God, he must possess true respect and fear of Him, the Creator and Sustainer of all things. Christians should exalt God because He does not require power and accomplishment from them. He only requires that they turn to Him in complete dependence.

Such songs as "Praise Ye the Lord, the Almighty," "O Worship the King" and "Guide Me, O Thou Great Jehovah" praise God's omnipotence. Other songs that praise God for the privilege of trusting Him are "Praise the Savior," "'Tis So Sweet to Trust in Jesus" and "Trusting Jesus."

The psalmist moves to a new subject in verses 12-20. In this third division he is careful to be thankful for Jehovah's blessing upon His Chosen People.

The Third Command to Sing

The admonition to praise the Lord (v. 12) was directed toward all of Jerusalem, referred to as Zion. The first command was directed toward singers without mention of the use of musical instruments. The second command was also directed toward individuals but included instrumental accompaniment. This third command is directed to an entire city. It involves great group singing.

The Reasons for Singing

The Holy Spirit turned the mind of the writer toward those blessings God pours out upon His children. A wide range of blessings is listed.

God's protection. When the gates of the city and bars of the gates were completed, the people of Jerusalem had a fresh feeling of security, especially when they played with their children inside the walls. Singing was a customary expression of security in Jerusalem.

A child of God today also experiences the protection of God. Some songs that help him express thanksgiving for it are "O God, Our Help in Ages Past," "A Child of the King" and "Leaning on the Everlasting Arms."

God's peace. Peace for the city of Jerusalem meant the end of threats from enemies. Fields were no longer ravaged and burned, crops grew to maturity, and abundance of food was everywhere (v. 14).

Songs of the church that express this peace include "Peace Like a River" and "I Am His and He Is Mine." While Christians are often battered and persecuted by the world, they should always be grateful for peace and plenty when they possess it.

God's promptness. The Word of God is characterized in verse 15 as being very swift. When God speaks a command, it is carried out without delay. The psalmist said, "His word runneth very swiftly," indicating the immediacy of Jehovah's response. This is strongly supported in the New Testament by such passages as Matthew 8:3, which tells how Jesus healed the man with leprosy: "And Jesus put forth his hand, and touched him, saying, I will; be thou clean. And immediately his leprosy was cleansed."

Those who desire to praise God for His continuous and swift watchcare may sing songs such as "Day by Day," "Each Step of the Way" and "I Just Keep Trusting My Lord."

God's perpetuity. God should be praised because He causes the seasons to come and go. The tilting of the earth on its axis and its wide path around the sun are no accident. God's commandment brings the snow and the ice in the fall and winter as well as the wind and warm rains of spring. Stanza 2 of "Great Is Thy Faithfulness" is an appropriate hymn of praise.

God's pronouncement. Psalm 147 concludes with a reminder that God has given a word of revelation to His people (vv. 19, 20). His unique Word serves as a standard for life and promise of hope for tomorrow. Its power to preserve and cleanse God's people must be extolled over and over again. Great songs of praises regarding God's Word are "Holy Bible, Book Divine," "The Divine Gift" and the all-time favorite "Standing on the Promises."

Are you praising God in song? Take time to review the reasons for praise given in this psalm. Find hymns and gospel choruses that accurately state these praises and sing them often in church and at home with your family. Praising God in song is good, refreshing and beautiful. It should be a part of every believer's life.

What Is Your Answer?

1. List some of the reasons the psalmist gives for praising the Lord.

2. What two attributes of God are mentioned by the psalmist in verse 5? How are they portrayed in this psalm?

3. List five of the Lord's works in nature, according to verses 8 and 9.

4. What weather or elements does God control (vv. 16, 17), and how does He control them (v. 18)?

5. What does the Lord show to Jacob, and what does He show to Israel?

6. According to verse 20, how can we know that Israel is special to God?

7. What similarity is there between the beginning and the end of this psalm?